HOME FOR CHRISTMAS

Home for Christmas:
Tales of Hope and Second Chances

Home for Christmas
978-1-5018-7044-6
978-1-5018-7045-3 *eBook*

Home for Christmas: DVD
978-1-5018-7048-4

Home for Christmas: Leader Guide
978-1-5018-7046-0
978-1-5018-7047-7 *eBook*

Home for Christmas: Youth Study Book
978-1-5018-7042-2
978-1-5018-7043-9 *eBook*

Foreword by Gregory Boyle

HOME FOR CHRISTMAS

TALES OF HOPE & SECOND CHANCES

JUSTIN COLEMAN

Abingdon Press / Nashville

Home for Christmas

Tales of Hope and Second Chances

Copyright © 2018 Abingdon Press
All rights reserved.

Library of Congress Cataloging-in-Publication data has been requested.

978-1-5018-7044-6

Scripture quotations are taken from the Common English Bible, copyright 2011. Used by permission. All rights reserved.

18 19 20 21 22 23 24 25 26 27 — 10 9 8 7 6 5 4 3 2 1
MANUFACTURED IN THE UNITED STATES OF AMERICA

*This book is dedicated to Chaka, Zan, Max,
and Lawson, who regularly remind me of
the gifts of home.*

CONTENTS

Acknowledgments 9

Foreword 13

Introduction 19

1. The Hope of New Life 27

2. The Love of the Last and the Lost 49

3. Your Joy Will Be Complete 75

4. Christ Is Our Peace 99

Conclusion 119

For Further Study 125

ACKNOWLEDGMENTS

There are so many people in my life who have made a resource like this possible.

My thanks go to the people of Homeboy Industries, particularly Father Greg Boyle, Norma Gilette, and Marissa Gilette, who first hosted me and introduced me to Homeboy, and to Alison Lass, who was so helpful as we put together this project.

I give thanks for the staff and people of University UMC in Chapel Hill, North Carolina, where this project was conceived. Thanks to our University UMC staff: Sharon Smith, Creighton Alexander, Tobi Nguyen, Laura Isaac, Tim Baker, Melissa Miller, Alice Anderson, Alison Haile, Betty Peterson, Brooke Davis, Kim Patterson, Manuel Wortman, Rebecca Dyck, Mike Saunders, John Samulski, Mary Yungeberg, Beth Alexander, Maung Kyar, and Lori Alvarez.

I would like to thank the people of St. Luke's United Methodist Church at both the Gethsemane and Westheimer campuses in Houston, Texas, who embraced and gave birth to the work of Houston reVision that was inspired by Homeboy Industries. Thanks to Tom Pace, Robbie McDonough, Mireya Ottaviano,

Erica Stark, Amy Kelley, Faith Ayers, Grady Light, Jasmine Young, Elizabeth Alvarado, Larry Moore, Linda Christians, Alice King, Corky and Chicky Fowler, and the many other staff members and congregants at St. Luke's UMC. Related to Houston reVision, I would like to thank Charles Rotramel and all of reVision's amazing staff members. I give thanks for the past and present members of Houston reVision's board: Gene Graham, Hank Coleman, Jeff Rawson, Stephen McCarthy, Bert Smith, Abbi Antablin, Kimberly McLeod, Paul Seernani, Barry Goldware, Robert Heston, Eric Moen, and Cliff Wright. Thanks to St. Martin's Episcopal Church and leaders within the Harris County Juvenile Probation Department who helped to give birth to Houston reVision.

Thanks to my father and mother, Austin and Elaine Coleman, and all of my siblings for their constant support and enthusiasm. Thanks to Rudy Rasmus, Jacob Breeze, Daniel Childs, Jason Burnham, Daniel Irving, Seann Duffin, Terence Hagans, Matt Rawle, Corie Wilkins, Janice Virtue, Bishop Janice Huie, Bishop Scott Jones, Bishop Hope Morgan Ward, Bishop Will Willimon, Stanley Hauerwas, Carol Goehring, Lawrence Young, Bill Gattis, Greg Jones, Neil Alexander, Dave Odom, Zan Holmes, Laura Nichol, and so many more friends and colleagues within The United Methodist Church and related institutions who have supported and encouraged me along the way.

Finally, I would like to thank all my friends at The United Methodist Publishing House. Particular thanks to Susan Salley and Maria Mayo, who believed in and championed this project from beginning to end. Thank you.

If you would like to support either of the wonderful nonprofits lifted up in this resource, they can be reached using the following contact information.

Houston reVision
6856 Bellaire Blvd.
Houston, TX 77074
https://www.houstonrevision.org/donate/

Homeboy Industries
130 W. Bruno St.
Los Angeles, CA 90012
https://www.homeboyindustries.org/donate/

FOREWORD

Meister Eckhart was a mystic and theologian who died in 1328. He said: "It is a lie, any talk of God that doesn't comfort you." Advent is this time of preparation. Clear the way. Make straight the path. Like John the Baptist alerting us to God's gentle arrival, we think we are supposed to remove the boulders in the road so that we can finally, in our upward ascent, reach this seemingly unreachable God. But God just longs to reach us, and yes, to comfort us.

I just buried my 92-year-old mother. She was not the least bit afraid of death. She was eager to join my father, who left us 22 years ago. "I can't wait to go home," she'd say. And then with exuberance and exhilaration, she would confide, "I've never *done* this before." It's something you would say before skydiving. Indeed, as she died—and I was so privileged to be the only one there, just the two of us—she let out this tiny, wondrous, glorious gasp, and then she left us. Skydiving. And no one in earshot of the sound could ever fear death again.

But in the last two weeks of her life, while one or two or eight of my siblings surrounded her bed, in her own home, she would

13

be in and out of consciousness, sometimes speaking a secret code known only to the dying. She'd awaken and then lock on to one of her kids and she'd say in breathless delight: "You're here! You're here!" Weeks later, I'd recall this and know that it reflected, in fact, the singular agenda item of our God. This spacious, expansive God of ours *only* wants to gaze at us, and with breathless delight, utter: "You're here. You're here." Behold the one beholding you and smiling. Notice the very notice of God. It is a lie, any talk of God that does not comfort us.

The Incarnation didn't happen because we are sinners and God became one of us as sort of a shock absorber between humanity and an angry God. The Incarnation happened because God's love needed to become tender. Jesus is the tenderness of God. Jean Vanier, the founder of the L'Arche communities, says that tenderness is spirituality at its most mature. At Homeboy Industries we say that love is the answer, community is the context, and tenderness is the methodology. For unless love becomes tender, it just settles somewhere in the ether or in the air or in our heads...or even in our hearts. But unless it becomes tender, there is no connective tissue that joins us to one another in God's dream come true: kinship. This is why Jesus came and what we prepare ourselves for in Advent.

Advent asks us to trade in the third-grade God we've settled for and exchange it for "the God who is always greater," as St. Ignatius tells us. So quite beyond the childish God we began with—the puny God who shakes his head, wags his finger, and is eternally disappointed at us for not measuring up—we surrender to the God of tenderness. This God has no enemies, only children. As a homie said to me once, "When God sees me, He doesn't see sin. He sees son." That's the God we actually have. Advent is about trading in the vindictive, disapproving God for the God who loves us without measure and without regret. This God does not share in the demonizing in which we all engage. This God shuns no one, ever, no exceptions. Advent is about allowing ourselves to be reached by the tenderness of God and then choosing to be that tenderness in the world.

I am sitting in my glass-enclosed office at our Homeboy Industries headquarters in Los Angeles's Chinatown. I can see the expanse of our reception area, teeming with gang members wanting to catch the crumb of hope that is falling from the table. They await tattoo removal, drug testing for our eighteen-month training program, an appointment with a therapist, or an anger-management class. Maybe they have signed up to see me. They will have to wait for a minute, since I'm with four prospective donors who just might help us fund our operation. Then I notice a gang member is at the front reception desk. I don't know him. He is waving a soda can and with each punctuation mark of his tirade to the homies behind the desk, big slurps of soda fly through the air. I know this is a combo-burger of meth and madness. There is clear discomfort telegraphed on our workers' faces. So I stand and begin to excuse myself from the donors to handle the situation.

Then I see Miguel, the head of our security team, walk up to this *vato* and put his arm around him and gently escort him outside. Miguel is the largest human being ever to work at Homeboy, huge and imposing. A gang member, he spent 21 years in prison, was a juvenile tried as an adult, and spent nearly half of his time in prison sequestered in solitary confinement. He just got cards made as the Head of Security, but he thought that title was too "highfalutin." So his cards read, "Community Outreach Worker." This felt more "humble" to him.

Later in the day, he told me what transpired with the "meth-madness" guy.

Miguel escorts the gentleman outside, and the man slowly lifts his T-shirt to reveal a gun tucked into the front of his pants. Then the guy drops the shirt. Miguel studies him gently. "How 'bout you and I go down to Olvera Street, and I'll buy you some tacos." The homie lifts his shirt again. Miguel looks him in the eyes. "Two tacos or three?"

And the guy agrees to walk the five blocks down Alameda to Olvera Street. "This poor guy," Miguel tells me later, "wasn't just listening to the voices in his head. The voices were leaping out of his mouth and he had a back and forth conversation with them."

"Shoot him."

"No, he's okay."

"Ya can't trust him."

"He's buying me tacos."

"And he went on and on like that," Miguel says, "till we got to the taco stand."

Miguel buys him three tacos. The man throws one taco to the ground with a decisive rage. Then he inhales the other two, ravenously and immediately.

Miguel is proof that only the soul who ventilates the world with tenderness has any chance of changing the world.

In this wonderful Advent study, Justin Coleman invites us all to allow free passage for the tender glance of God to reach us and transform us from the inside out. We marinate in the lavish affection of our God, who doesn't want anything *from* us, only *for* us. To know that about our spacious and expansive God is to feel compelled to be God's tenderness in the world. We can do no other. Prepare the way. Make straight the path. The tenderness of God reaches us, and all we want to do is to be in the world, to be who God is: compassionate, with loving-kindness.

This beautiful book helps us hear better the only words God longs to utter, with breathless delight: "You're here. You're here." Comfort. At long last.

Gregory Boyle
Los Angeles, California
May 2018

INTRODUCTION

Coming home. It sounds like something we do every day, something that most of us take for granted: opening our door and returning to our own space, a safe place. It's an idea that has everything to do with Advent, a time when we remember the home in God we are always invited to return to. It's a time of hope and expectation, of joy and thanksgiving for the home we're offered, the home we're reminded of in the birth of Jesus.

But for so many people, home is far from certain; it may be a concept so unfamiliar it's impossible to hope for it. This is especially true during the Christmas season, when it seems to a lot of us that everyone else has a happy family, a place to go. And for people who have experienced brokenness in their homes, for those who live in poverty and situations of violence, home, if the physical place exists, may be a nightmare. For many young people in East Los Angeles, the reality of gangs and a lack of resources make the thought of home something less than pleasant. It's easy for these children of God, born into conditions of structural violence, racism, and poverty, to live without hope. That's why this Advent study is looking at a place that's changing things for people who have sometimes been without homes or family or a friendly or safe place to be in this world.

For the past thirty years, Homeboy Industries has been working to provide young people in violent and under-resourced parts of Los Angeles with a home, and with the hope that comes along with it. The largest gang intervention and post-incarceration rehabilitation and re-entry program in the world, Homeboy works each year with more than 8,000 individuals who are looking for hope and second chances.

When he was a new priest in East Los Angeles, Homeboy's founder, Father Gregory Boyle, realized that the area's young gang members were suffering from what he calls "a lethal absence of hope."[1] He decided to combat that lack by providing this community with the economic, material, emotional, and spiritual resources required for its people and places not only to survive, but to thrive—to make an area dismissed as hopeless into a vibrant and mutually supportive home. Ever since, Homeboy has offered services such as tattoo removal, education, anger-management and substance-abuse classes, counseling, legal help, and job training. Homeboy businesses, which include silk screening, the Homeboy Bakery, and the Homegirl Cafe, give participants job skills that will translate into a productive life outside Homeboy Industries. And the entire enterprise has the feel of an intimate home, where participants come together in celebration, support, and kinship.

As we hear the stories of the homeboys and homegirls who have found new life and new possibilities through Homeboy Industries, we'll see what Advent means, what it offers to all of us,

---

1   Gregory Boyle, *Barking to the Choir: The Power of Radical Kinship* (New York: Simon & Schuster, 2017), 130–131.

not only for a single season, but throughout the rest of our lives as well. As we look at participants' lives alongside Scripture, we'll learn not only what we're given in Advent, but also what we are called to give one another: the hope, love, joy, and peace—the new home—God offers us all.

I gave you a general introduction to what Homeboy Industries is about—but I want to let you in on a fuller picture of exactly what goes on there, so that you can keep in mind how this place exemplifies the aspects of Christian life made so evident during Advent.

I first came to Homeboy on a research trip when I was a pastor in southwest Houston. My church in Texas was located in a neutral zone between two areas experiencing high levels of juvenile gang activity. Wanting to address the needs of the area, and to try to bring some peace and healing to the people who lived there, some other church members and I joined in with a group from an Episcopal church we were partnered with to see what we could do. As we researched how other religious organizations around the country were addressing similar situations, we were surprised to find that very few of them could point to the strong redemptive track record that Homeboy had. And so it made sense for our group to seek advice from the clear leader of organizations working with juvenile gang members. We travelled from Houston to Los Angeles looking for hope, and we found it in the lives and stories of Father Gregory Boyle and those we encountered at Homeboy Industries.

In addition to Boyle, other Jesuits work among those receiving help at Homeboy, living out a call to offer hope and a home to the homeboys and homegirls who need them. Those served by Homeboy Industries—employees who are called "homies" within the organization—include former gang members who have not only demonstrated amazing resilience in overcoming difficult pasts and facing up to challenging presents, but have also displayed great leadership abilities. Some of these homies have become senior staff members, or serve as leaders in other key program areas such as outreach and substance-abuse counseling. And then you have even more people who have given up what might have been more lucrative opportunities in other places because of the spirit and love and meaning they find at Homeboy. They see God in the faces of each of these homies. I've seen these and other staff members at Homeboy live out the message of something one of my childhood pastors used to say: "Behind the face of every person is the face of God, and how you treat every person is how you treat God." Because they see God in the people who walk through their doors, the people at Homeboy pour out their lives into the lives of the homeboys and homegirls—and those homeboys and homegirls turn right around and pour out their lives into those of the staff. What you see happening at Homeboy is an embodiment of wonderful mutuality and hope—an embodiment of home.

A day at Homeboy begins with a brief morning meeting. Everyone in the building gathers in the central lobby and around the balcony and stairs. The environment has the feel of an intimate home, and the meeting itself gives the impression of a family gathering. Getting together in the morning involves everything from celebrating (birthdays, the end of a participant's probation period, and so on) to reviewing practical and logistical issues associated with running the center to a review of the day's calendar, where you also learn which outside groups will be touring the site that day.

The most powerful part of this brief meeting is the thought for the day. Usually delivered by Father Gregory Boyle—who's known among the homies as "G-Dog," "Father G," or simply "G"— the message might also be offered by a staff member or one of the homies. The thought for the day is really a homily, whose themes generally have to do with hope, redemption, second chances, and kinship. These homilies are simultaneously testimony and sermon. The stories are real, the transformation is clear, and the love that is felt is all encompassing. One of Father Boyle's messages involved a reminder to everyone at the meeting that happiness is trying to find us, that God is trying to find us—but that we can't see it, or let ourselves be found, because we're not in touch with our own wounds and brokenness. We don't even know what's making us unhappy, so there's no way we can recognize happiness trying to get our attention. When Father Boyle closed his message with the call to "Let yourself be found," it was a communication of exactly what happens at Homeboy: working to get to the root of the community's wounds, so that they can know them, address them, and let happiness find them.[2]

When you listen to the thought for the day, standing among Homeboy staff and participants, all of a sudden you realize that in the midst of a large lobby that could be the entrance to any business complex, you are really at church. An everyday liturgy is being lived out before you. The community has gathered, they have been called together, the familiar verses of their lives are being read, there is a message, and there is prayer. The whole

---

2   Let Yourself Be Found, Thought for the Day for October 23, 2017, from Gregory Boyle, Homeboy Industries, https://www.homeboyindustries.org/thought-of-the-day/.

building embodies a call to confession and a pronouncement of forgiveness all at once. Even after the meeting, you can go right next door to Homegirl Cafe and break bread together as you are served communion in the form of a breakfast, lunch, or dinner prepared with food that's come straight from the farm to your table. As you and those around you enjoy a meal inspired by the Latino cultures in the neighborhood, you realize that Homeboy is a reminder of who the Church is when it's at its best.

If you are a guest visiting for the day, you can arrange for a tour. Here, visitors are paired with a homie who will guide them through the facility and share a bit about themselves—their personal testimony—along the way. I've been on several of these tours, and each has been incredibly moving. The homies share stories of neighborhood struggles, abandonment, trauma, and abuses of all sorts—both abuses inflicted upon them and abuses they have inflicted upon others. In these stories, you begin to see the seductive pull of gang life. You are promised safety, protection, a new family. But even though most of what you get in a gang is more pain, the call of gang life is easy to understand if you imagine yourself growing up in similar conditions—if you allow yourself to realize just what these conditions entail, and then try to imagine how you would try to deal with them. Gregory Boyle writes, "Here is what we seek: a compassion that can stand in awe at what the poor have to carry rather than stand in judgment at how they carry it."[3] I am a witness who stands in awe.

My wish for you as you go through this Advent study is that the stories of Homeboy participants will open you up to new,

---

3   Gregory Boyle, *Tattoos on the Heart: The Power of Boundless Compassion* (New York: Free Press, 2010), 67.

fuller, deeper understandings of the home God offers us. I pray you will see that that home is filled with a thrilling hope grounded in the certainty of new life God offers us in Christ. I want you to experience God's tender, steadfast love that always wins out over judgment, and will always offer us another chance, no matter how many times we've failed before. As you read, I hope you will experience the grateful joy of God's love for you, and carry that joy into your relationships with friends, family, and everyone in your community. And by the time you come to the end of this book, I hope that you will have found the full, all-encompassing peace we find in God, the peace that gives us the courage and strength to carry on with confidence, even when it seems nothing is going our way and nothing stays the same. And in all these things, my wish is that you share this home God offers us—especially with those who believe they have no home and no hope. My wish is that you make Advent and Christmas a time to practice this opening of hopeful doors with every person who comes your way—to do what Christ has done for us. May the hope, love, joy, and peace of Christ be with you. Welcome home!

Chapter 1

THE HOPE OF NEW LIFE

Chapter 1

The Hope of New Life

I offer my life to you, Lord.
> *My God, I trust you.*
Please don't let me be put to shame!
> *Don't let my enemies rejoice over me!*
For that matter,
> *don't let anyone who hopes in you*
>> *be put to shame;*
> *instead, let those who are treacherous without*
> *excuse be put to shame.*

Make your ways known to me, Lord;
> *teach me your paths.*
Lead me in your truth—teach it to me—
> *because you are the God who saves me.*
>> *I put my hope in you all day long.*

*Lord, remember your compassion and faithful love—
    they are forever!
But don't remember the sins of my youth or my
wrongdoing.
        Remember me only according to your faithful love
            for the sake of your goodness, Lord.*

*The Lord is good and does the right thing;
    he teaches sinners which way they should go.
God guides the weak to justice,
    teaching them his way.
All the Lord's paths are loving and faithful
    for those who keep his covenant and laws.*

Psalm 25:1-10

JENNIFER: THE HOPE OF HOME

It was the beginning of December, and Jennifer was incarcerated. Separated from her two small children, she spent Christmas facing the possibility of up to thirty-eight years in prison. After agreeing to a plea deal and arranging to live with her mother, Jennifer began working at Homeboy Industries. At first, everything was great; she and her children were making a new life together. But then her mother kicked the entire family out of the house. After such a promising start, Jennifer and her two children were homeless, and she felt like giving up and returning to her past life, and to the drugs and alcohol that had been part of it.

But Homeboy Industries came to Jennifer's assistance, helping her to find a transitional housing program. Able now to pay her rent, Jennifer has started college, and was also able to spend this past Christmas with her children. Not only have the community and support—her new home at Homeboy—given Jennifer this second chance at life, but also she says the love that she finds in and from her new, second family "actually gives me a lot of hope."

THE HOPE OF CHRIST

Do you know what song was the first to be played on the radio? On the evening of December 24, 1906, Reginald Fessenden, a Canadian-born inventor who had once worked for Thomas Edison, was experimenting with what was known as "wireless telegraphy," or radio. He read from Luke 2, played with some vinyl records, and then picked up his violin and started to play a hymn, "O Holy Night."

It begins this way (emphasis added):

> O holy night! the stars are brightly shining;
> It is the night of the dear Savior's birth.
> Long lay the world in sin and error pining,
> Till he appeared and **the soul felt its worth**.

and continues:

> **A thrill of hope**—the weary world rejoices,
> For yonder breaks a new and glorious morn!

I know what some of you are saying to yourselves. "That's a Christmas song. Why is he talking about a Christmas song at the beginning of a book about Advent? Advent is a time where we prepare for Christ's birth. We need to keep from mentioning Christmas until, well, Christmas. No spoilers!"

I must tell you that I've never had someone say to me on Christmas Eve, "Wait! What? This is about the birth of Jesus?!?

31

I did *not* see that one coming." Knowing what's coming provides a good reminder that we need to hold a more expansive view of the season. We move into Advent reminding ourselves of what God has done and is doing in the lives of God's children and God's world. Advent and Christmastide—and the entire liturgical year, for that matter—aren't just points we follow, one to the next, on a straight line. The liturgical cycle is precisely that: a cycle, where events and people and situations flow back into one another in an ever-changing web of relationships.

The hymn captures the feeling of this ever-renewed build toward the excitement of Christmas: "A thrill of hope." I love that phrase. We talk about many feelings related to hope, but I don't often hear people speak of the thrill of it.

That might be due to the ways many of us experience the concept of hope today, when we "hope" for things that are desired, but not real or attainable. We speak of hope as if we should not hold our breath believing that for which we hope will come true. We say things like, "Don't get your hopes up" and, "Don't reach too high because you might fall." This sort of hope is ungrounded because it never expects to enter into reality. Hope defined this way is nothing more than a fanciful wish or dream.

But this is not how Scripture talks about hope. In Scripture, hope is something that is both desired and possible. In fact, it is not only possible, it is expected. For hope to move beyond a wish or dream, it has to become grounded in some deep understanding and belief about our world and how it works, both physically and spiritually. And when we understand the cycles our liturgy helps make present, that grounded hope contains an excitement, the thrill of knowing that immense good is on the horizon but that we may have only an inkling about the forms that hope will take. When we are grounded in possibilities, our hope is thrilled by the suspense of waiting for the surprising forms in which it will be fulfilled.

Hope is something that is both desired and possible. In fact, it is not only possible, it is expected.

My hope is grounded in new life. That is to say, my hope is grounded in a theology of creation and new creation. These images bookend the Christian Bible. Scripture begins with creation—God making everything and calling it good. What follows is a sometimes-messy middle portion of Scripture where humanity struggles to return to the goodness we once experienced in the Garden of Eden, not knowing the shapes that goodness will take. In time, we see the advent of Christ and the possibility of becoming a new creation. As 2 Corinthians 5:17 says, "If anyone is in Christ, that person is part of the new creation. The old things have gone away, and look, new things have arrived!" Finally, in the book of Revelation, we see a picture of the fulfillment of this work of new creation as God renews, restores, and resurrects everything. This is our picture of Christian hope. God gives all of creation a second chance. Maybe one of the most famous examples of a second chance from the New Testament is the conversion of the Apostle Paul. Until he was confronted with the spirit of Christ along the highway, the person then known as Saul was doing everything he could to persecute the followers of Jesus. Why should God have given him, of all people, a second chance? But not only did that second chance result in a change of heart and name, but also that person who seemed past redemption is also the one who wrote a large part of the Scriptures we now use to understand who God is.

Even when we move away from well-known stories of hope and reconciliation, out into the mess of the real world, my hope is grounded in this new life, this sense of creation and new creation from God. I feel hopeful when I see a child born, knowing it hasn't yet experienced any of the evils of this world, and that it has its whole life ahead of it, ready to grow in surprising ways. I feel hopeful when I see a sprout of new life from a garden, the creation of a beautiful new piece of art, or someone baptized. All new creation. All good. All just what God had in mind. During the Advent and Christmas season, it's not just that we hope Christ will save us or that we hope Christ will return, but that we enter into Christian community expecting new life. Some speak of Advent as a season of generic waiting, as if we were only waiting for Christmas presents or waiting to play Christmas music. But waiting in itself is not quite enough for me. Advent is about waiting with a sense of longing and expectation. We enter into Advent expectantly, trusting that Jesus will come again, and longing for the renewal that Christ brings.

Our hopes may be dashed, of course. And we know that even the dreams we have for children can be crushed by poverty, violence, disease, and more. As these children become adults, the only options they may have are directed at mere survival; they do what they can to stay alive and to support those who depend on them, whether that means working three low-wage jobs or dealing drugs to pay the rent. For those who have lost their share of hope, their ability to be expectant, Homeboy Industries provides new life that reinjects that hope into their world.

LEARNING TO LIVE CHRIST'S HOPE

One of Homeboy's taglines says that it is a place where "hope has an address." I love this image. It strikes me that every church should be able to claim that it is hope's residence. Hope has an address in places where people are actively talking about what it means to be incarnational witnesses to hope: engaging in meaningful action that creates room for people to find paths to love and grace—paths to second chances. We all need second chances.

Part of what I find hopeful in the ministry that we encounter at Homeboy Industries and in the stories that make up the place is what Boyle calls the "'no matter whatness' of God."[1] This is the idea that God loves you no matter what, and that when you are among the people of God, we are going to love you into newness of life. This sounds so good. It sounds so easy. But, in fact, I think this is one of the hardest parts of the gospel to learn and to live out. We have this sneaking suspicion that God may not love us no matter what. We've heard too many Christians condemn people— for their sexual orientation, for failed relationships, for struggles with addiction—so that we're often led to believe that God looms above us with a hammer, as if life were one big cosmic game of

---

1   Gregory Boyle, *Tattoos on the Heart: The Power of Boundless Compassion* (New York: Free Press, 2010), 52.

whack-a-mole. But if we were to trust, on the other hand, in this "no matter whatness" and believe that this is how we are loved—unconditionally—we would also have to do the hard work of loving others in similar fashion. It is simply easier, for example, to judge or act out against those who have offended us than to trust that the tender, loving kindness of God will transform us and offer us hope.

Now, at least periodically, all of us suffer from what I think of as a hope gap—the difference between our lived experience, our reality, and what we hope for. You might just say that we're disappointed in our hopes. And we all hope at different levels. Some people hope to go to college, to land a good job, or to start a family. But others hope for basic needs like food, clothing, and shelter—hopes that many of us are lucky enough not to have experienced or even have thought of. And this is where hope gaps overlap with opportunity gaps, the lack of opportunities in life due to structural poverty or racism or violence, or to the absence of the security loving parents or family or a good education can provide. As Father Boyle says about the unequal chances people have in life, "not all choices are created equal. And a person's ability to choose is not created equal."[2] When you have a choice between no family at all and the family a gang provides, your choices are limited—and unequal to those most of us enjoy.

But instead of understanding that some people make bad choices because they have no others, we tend to abandon hope for those people altogether. In fact, we often talk about people and

---

2   Gregory Boyle, "The Calling of Delight: Gangs, Service, and Kinship," interview by Krista Tippett, *On Being*, The On Being Project, April 2, 2015, audio, 50:59, https://onbeing.org/programs/greg-boyle-the-calling-of-delight-gangs-service-and-kinship/.

places suffering from an opportunity gap as being godforsaken. God, though, doesn't forsake people or places. And if we're to be God's church, we can't take the easy route and dismiss economically depressed or violence-ridden communities as hopeless—as bereft of God's presence. If we are to believe in the hope God offers us, we have to extend that hope to those broken places as well.

Not all choices are created equal. And a person's ability to choose is not created equal.
—Father Gregory Boyle

HOPE IN HARD PLACES

Now, I don't know how much you know about the prophet Jeremiah. In his zeal to call his people to faithful living in God, he went to some pretty interesting extremes. We might call a lot of what he did performance art, walking around with an ox's yoke around his neck, say, to make a point. But he also used what even then was commonly recognized media: in this instance, he wrote a letter. Here's part of what it said:

> The LORD of heavenly forces, the God of Israel, proclaims to all the exiles I have carried off from Jerusalem to Babylon: Build houses and settle down; cultivate gardens and eat what they produce. Get

married and have children; then help your sons find wives and your daughters find husbands in order that they too may have children. Increase in number there so that you don't dwindle away. Promote the welfare of the city where I have sent you into exile. Pray to the LORD for it, because your future depends on its welfare.

The LORD of heavenly forces, the God of Israel, proclaims: Don't let the prophets and diviners in your midst mislead you. Don't pay attention to your dreams. They are prophesying lies to you in my name. I didn't send them, declares the LORD.

The LORD proclaims: When Babylon's seventy years are up, I will come and fulfill my gracious promise to bring you back to this place. I know the plans I have in mind for you, declares the LORD; they are plans for peace, not disaster, to give you a future filled with hope. When you call me and come and pray to me, I will listen to you. When you search for me, yes, search for me with all your heart, you will find me. I will be present for you, declares the LORD, and I will end your captivity. I will gather you from all the nations and places where I have scattered you, and I will bring you home after your long exile, declares the LORD.

Jeremiah 29:4-14

Let's stop for a moment and imagine where Jeremiah was coming from. Let's think about who it was he was talking to. Why all this talk about marrying and settling down? Wasn't that always the point: to lead a good life in God's community?

The sixth century BC, when Jeremiah wrote his letter, was a pretty low time for the Kingdom of Judah—the southern half of what had once been a united Israelite kingdom. The whole region had been subject to the Babylonians for quite a while, all of it forced to pay tribute to what amounted to foreign and unwelcome rulers. The people of Judah, including their king, weren't very happy with the situation, and there had been some minor rebellions going on—small uprisings which, for the most part, the Babylonians had ignored, not seeing them as all that threatening or important. After all, they were a great power, and the little region of Judah didn't count for much in the grand scheme of things.

But then the king went too far. He made it about income, and refused to pay the tribute he owed the Babylonians to ensure a peaceful existence—a payment that worked along the same lines as a high-level, not-quite-mutually agreeable form of protection money that a mob boss would understand.

After all the rebellions, the Babylonians decided that little Judah had gone too far—and so they went in and showed the rest of the region what happened to little kingdoms that wouldn't obey their rulers. The Babylonians destroyed the Temple in Jerusalem. They destroyed the city's walls and its houses and took the kingdom's leaders and most important citizens away from their home, into exile in Babylon, where they could be watched over more carefully. The peasants were left behind to do the best they could without religious or civil leaders, without a social system, without much of anything at all.

The Babylonians saw this practice of leveling a place and exiling its people as a way of scattering former enemies to the winds, removing them from their homes—from their bases and networks of power and support and comfort—so that they would be left disconnected and dispersed and eventually cease to exist as a unified nation able to take any meaningful action against their rulers.

This is the situation Jeremiah is writing about and to: a community that found itself in a place not its home, with everything they had known destroyed. In other words, utterly hopeless. But they were also determined not to let the Babylonians' intentions for them prevail; they were determined to keep themselves together and to maintain their unique identity as a people, one that would never accept the attempt that had been made to wipe them out. They were, in other words, trying to stay faithful to who they were, in a situation where it seemed impossible to do it. They were trying to stay faithful to God, in a place that didn't seem to know or want to hear about God at all.

It was hard to hope in these conditions, so far away from home, amid strangers and at the mercy of hostile rulers. It was hard to hope that, if they *were* able to return, there would be anything left for them. Would they have a home to go back to? Would others have turned it into *their* home? Would those who had been allowed to stay recognize the returning exiles anymore—or worse? Would they accuse them of having sold out, abandoned, and given up on those who had stayed behind? If they decided to make the best of a bad situation in Babylon—if they found work, found someone there to start a family with, found some way to make the experience in exile livable—would they be called traitors once they returned?

It may have seemed as if every answer was the wrong one, and that the best thing to do was sit and accept the misery of their fate. This way, at least, they would still be themselves, and no one, especially God, could accuse them of being otherwise. But Jeremiah speaks directly to their fears, and shows them that God knows what they're going through.

The prophet speaks of a hope filled with anticipation; he allows the exiles to hope that they *will* be able to survive, and even thrive, until they are brought home again, without fearing the condemnation of others. And within this reassurance is contained the greatest hope-filled anticipation of all: the hope that they *will* return, plain and simple—that God will bring them home.

There probably isn't any part of their situation that they could've predicted—not how they got there, not what Babylon is like, and not how or whether they will ever be able to return home. But they should be assured—they should keep hope alive—Jeremiah tells them, because even though they don't know exactly *how* it will happen, this exile *will* come to an end. The community taken out of Jerusalem against their will *will* return home.

Indeed, God did bring the exiles back home from Babylon. When the Persian King Cyrus defeated the Babylonians, one of his official acts was to allow this group of Jewish leaders to return to Jerusalem. They probably couldn't have predicted such a thing would happen, or that their deliverance would come from God through yet another foreign ruler—but as Jeremiah had told them it would be, their hope—their anticipation—was vindicated.

BRINGING IT HOME: HOPE IN SCRIPTURE

You can hear the psalmist's longing in the verse that started our chapter. There is some deep need that is being expressed. Life is coming at the psalmist hard, and there is concern that if the oppositional forces win, the psalmist will be put to shame. But the concern here is not only for the individual; the concern is for all who hope in God. The psalmist pleads in verse 3: "don't let anyone who hopes in you / be put to shame."

Verse 4 reads, "Make your ways known to me, LORD; / teach me your paths." During Advent, we hear the cry of the prophet to prepare a way for the Lord by making paths straight (Isaiah 40:3, Mark 1:3)—or as some translations have it, "level" or "smooth." The psalmist is asking the Lord to teach us the paths to God's love and grace that are smooth and that can be navigated without obstruction. As has been the case with many Homeboy participants, we sometimes choose paths that lead us away from God's love and grace—treacherous paths that lead us into hopelessness rather than hope. And when there is no hope, people often wander into life- and soul-threatening situations—drug or alcohol abuse, membership in a gang—as they seek to compensate for or numb their pain. But if the soul can find its way to paths of love and grace, all of a sudden, a new life appears—all of a sudden, there is hope.

The psalmist writes:

> Lead me in your truth—teach it to me—
>> because you are the God who saves me.
>>> I put my hope in you all day long.
> LORD, remember your compassion and faithful love—
>> they are forever!
> But don't remember the sins of my youth or my wrongdoing.
>> Remember me only according to your faithful love
>>> for the sake of your goodness, LORD.
>>>> *Psalms 25:5-7*

Compassion and God's faithful or steadfast love are the catalyst of hope in the Christian life. Compassion and faithful love are part of the tenderness that God extends toward us that softens our hardened hearts and makes paths smooth so that the love of God can reach us in an increasing number of ways.

Part of Homeboy's work involves offering gang members the compassion and faithful love they have never had. Father Boyle talks about young people whose parents or caregivers may only have been there for them in frightening ways. And so, not only did they never experience a calming influence in tense or violent situations, but they also learned they could never let their guard down, that it was never safe to accept or offer kindness to anyone, even to oneself—that sometimes, the safest thing to do was hurt others before you got hurt. One of the things Homeboy offers, then, is "attachment repair," learning to be together in—to feel safe in—mutual kinship and support.[3] It's the kind of family Christian communities are called to offer each other, the same kind of mutual vulnerability among its members that allows hope to thrive and new life to emerge.

In Jennifer's case, that sort of hope gives her something to fight for. She knows she's not in the clear yet, and that it will be hard to complete her education and to raise her kids. But the hope she's found at Homeboy gives her the courage to keep working for the life she wants. Instead of the helplessness that comes along with a sense of hopelessness, Jennifer can now see the possibility of new life, whereas no life could be seen before. It is the exciting possibility of new life in Christ—of being a new creation. This is living into the thrill of hope.

---

3   Boyle, "The Calling of Delight."

As another Christmas draws near, Jennifer knows that being able to spend it with her kids isn't the only thing she has—she also has an entire loving, supportive community holding her up at every time of the year, offering her new life and an always-new creation. As we approach Christmas, let us give thanks for the people who hold us up—and let us be the kinds of people, the communities, who offer the same support and love that allow hope to be born and grow.

DEVOTION

Our souls long for hope. We are simply not made for hopelessness. Hope is an amazing gift to a world that is sometimes weary. Weariness sometimes leads to hopelessness. It is perfectly natural to feel sad sometimes. Sadness is a part of life, but hopelessness does not need to be.

My hope is grounded in new life. When I think of new life I cannot help thinking of Scriptures that speak to newness of life in Christ, like 2 Corinthians 5:17: "So then, if anyone is in Christ, that person is part of the new creation. The old things have gone away, and look, new things have arrived!"

Hope is grounded in the picture of new life that we see in Scripture. New things have arrived in our lives in Christ and this newness offers us a thrill of hope. There is a new genesis going on in each of our souls, taking any weariness and hopelessness that may be found there and transforming them into a refreshed hopefulness.

New things are arriving in Christ now and more newness of life is yet to come. Think about the picture we see in Revelation 21:

Then I saw a new heaven and a new earth,
for the former heaven and the former earth

had passed away, and the sea was no more.
I saw the holy city, New Jerusalem, coming
down out of heaven from God, made ready as
a bride beautifully dressed for her husband. I
heard a loud voice from the throne say, "Look!
God's dwelling is here with humankind. He
will dwell with them, and they will be his
peoples. God himself will be with them as
their God. He will wipe away every tear from
their eyes. Death will be no more. There will
be no mourning, crying, or pain anymore, for
the former things have passed away." Then
the one seated on the throne said, "Look! I'm
making all things new."

Revelation 21:1-5

Life can be hard sometimes. The circumstances of our lives can make our souls weary, but don't be discouraged. Through the work of the Holy Spirit, God is working in us and through us and around us to make things new. This work of God sometimes takes time. New life often grows in stages, but we can trust that God is with us every step along the journey.

Remember God's word to us from the prophet Isaiah:

Look! I'm doing a new thing;
*   now it sprouts up; don't you recognize it?*

I'm making a way in the desert,
   paths in the wilderness.

                              Isaiah 43:19

God of all creation, by your mercy, renew and restore us. Help us to be a people who are born anew in Christ. May the newness of life that we receive in Christ give us hope and may we be a sign of hope to the world. Amen.

Chapter 2

THE LOVE OF THE LAST AND THE LOST

Chapter 2

THE LOVE OF THE LAST AND THE LOST

I thank my God every time I mention you in my prayers. I'm thankful for all of you every time I pray, and it's always a prayer full of joy. I'm glad because of the way you have been my partners in the ministry of the gospel from the time you first believed it until now. I'm sure about this: the one who started a good work in you will stay with you to complete the job by the day of Christ Jesus. I have good reason to think this way about all of you because I keep you in my heart. You are all my partners in God's grace, both during my time in prison and in the defense and support of the gospel. God is my witness that I feel affection for all of you with the compassion of Christ Jesus.

This is my prayer: that your love might become even more and more rich with knowledge and all kinds of insight. I pray this so that you will be able to decide what really matters and so you will be sincere and blameless on the day of Christ. I pray that you will then be filled with the fruit of righteousness, which comes from Jesus Christ, in order to give glory and praise to God.

Philippians 1:3-11

CARL: THE LOVE OF COMMUNITY

Carl admits that the atmosphere at Homeboy Industries might be a little disorienting to visitors, who are probably used to seeing tattoos and thinking, "Gangs! Danger!" Visitors may expect the homeboys and homegirls to give them "some type of look" demanding to know why they're there—may expect anything but the loving welcome they receive when they walk through the doors. Carl says it's the evident kinship at Homeboy that helped him learn how to communicate with other people—and how to love both them and himself. "That's love for me," he says: the fact that this place has brought together onetime enemies and turned them into family.

THE LOVE OF CHRIST

We talked in the last chapter about the theme of hope that runs through the hymn "O Holy Night." Well, that familiar song has more to say about what God's love means for us, both during Advent and throughout the year. As the song's third verse has it,

> Truly he taught us to love one another;
> His law is love and his gospel is peace.

Of course, we also hear a lot in the Bible about love; one of the central affirmations of the Christian faith is that God is love. As 1 John 4:8 has it, "The person who doesn't love does not know God, because God is love." And I'm sure you've heard so many other examples of the importance of love in Scripture. We say that God loved the world so much that God gave God's only begotten Son so that we might be saved (John 3:16). And in John 13:34-35, not only are we told that Jesus taught his disciples that they would be known by their love for one another, but we also see that our call to love each other is not merely a suggestion on the part of Jesus—it is a new commandment. We probably need to receive this call to love in this imperative form—because as Luke 6:32 reminds us, loving as generously as God loves is no easy task. Anyone can love those they already love or those they are most inclined to love. As Jesus says to his disciples in this verse, " 'If you love those who love you, why should you be commended? Even sinners love those who love them.' " Even sinners can muster enough love to love those who love them, but the followers of Jesus are called to more.

And this *more* doesn't only take the form of a commandment; we see the centrality of love for Christian life when Jesus describes it as the heart of the Law as well. In Matthew 22:34-40, a legal expert from a group of Pharisees asks Jesus, "Teacher, what is the greatest commandment in the Law?" Jesus replies:

> "You must love the Lord your God with all your
> heart, with all your being, *and with all your mind.*
> *This is the first and greatest commandment. And*

the second is like it: You must love your neighbor
as you love yourself. *All the Law and the Prophets
depend on these two commands."*

Matthew 22:37-40

Love seems to be the interpretive key that Jesus exhorts us to use as we consider the Law. Many Bibles call this exhortation a new commandment based on John 13:34, noted above. But in Matthew, Jesus' charge appears to be more of an encouragement to deepen our understanding of the commandments, or a clarification of those commandments—the very commandments that make up the Law.

We need this deeper understanding—this love—because without it, what is the Law except a set of rules to follow? These rules might maintain some kind of order in life, but without love, will they create newness or wholeness in life? These questions ought to make us ask others: What is the Church if it is not loving? What are rules for in the Church if they aren't loving? Can such a church without love still be the Church? We can go further and ask questions like this: What is a service project if it is not motivated by love? What is Christmas if there is no love among the people you spend it with? What is home if love cannot be found there?

In order to answer these questions, we need to know what it means to love. After all, it's easy to say we should love one another; it's even easy to understand that this commandment forms an essential part of the Law God has intended for us. But what do these assertions all mean, when you get right down to it? How do we show love in our actual interactions with each other? We need good definitions of love.

First Corinthians 13 highlights some of the many dimensions of love:

> *Love is patient, love is kind, it isn't jealous, it doesn't*
> *brag, it isn't arrogant, it isn't rude, it doesn't seek*
> *its own advantage, it isn't irritable, it doesn't keep*
> *a record of complaints, it isn't happy with injustice,*
> *but it is happy with the truth. Love puts up with*
> *all things, trusts in all things, hopes for all things,*
> *endures all things. Love never fails.*
>
> *1 Corinthians 13:4-8a*

For this chapter, the aspect of love that most stands out is patience. In the midst of a transformation process, a lack of patience may fall short of the high calling to love. If we expect instant turnarounds in people's behavior or affections, our disappointment may cause us to abandon our goodwill and commitment toward another person. Christ coming into the world provides us an example not only of the redemptive action or direct intervention of God, but also of the patience of God, who journeys with us, puts up with us, and suffers with us—who gives us one second chance after another and never gets fed up and calls it quits—all because God loves us. This sort of love endures all things—and it simply never fails.

There's a problem, though. Even though the centrality of love for Christian life seems pretty clear-cut, so does the Christian concern for sin—specifically, for ridding the world of sin. At a couple places where I've worked, we have done major renovations of spaces. Some of those spaces have required an abatement process to create a safe environment for workers and those who would eventually inhabit those spaces. I'm always impressed by the fact that the Church is in the sin-abatement business. We work to diminish sin and the effects of sin in the lives of those who believe.

And so the Church talks about ways to remove the effects of sin from the world—about the best way to carry out the sin-abatement business. There are at least a couple of approaches to this work that the Church might take. One is to judge or discipline sin's effects out of this world. This posture says that if we discipline people—if we judge between what is good and bad or right and wrong in the life of an individual or community, then we might offer enough of a corrective that the individual and/or community would become free of sin's effects. This position is like a bloodhound tracking down sin—always seeking to sniff sin out. When this sin is found, the bloodhound bites in and doesn't let go until it gets the result it wants.

Sometimes we are so fixed on being right and pointing out wrongdoing that we miss the mark of the high call of God in Jesus Christ to love the sin out of the world.

Trying to judge sin out of the world is not meant to be a malicious activity. This kind of practice is meant to act as a form of accountability, or a discipline that leads to righteousness. But the Church can so easily wound people. My experience is that

Christians tend to carry this idea that God sent that inflection of God's self that is the Son into the world to right wrongs—particularly the wrong of sin. To a certain degree this is true. Jesus' ministry does involve setting aright wrong thinking and actions so that the wrong can be made right or made new. But sometimes we are so fixed on being right and pointing out wrongdoing that we miss the mark of the high call of God in Jesus Christ to love the sin out of the world.

I once had a college student ask me why some Christian people were so judgmental. I replied that I thought it is because we sometimes get out of touch with our own brokenness. We often act as if we have always lived our Christian lives perfectly, or at least as if we have always lived them better than the people we are tempted to judge. But if we were in touch with our pain—the pain of *not* living into our lives as perfectly as we would have liked, the pain of having made bad decisions or missing out on resources or experiences we craved—we would have a greater sense of empathy for the pain of others. Simply recalling how it feels when we ourselves have failed to live up to our own or others' expectations—or how it feels when others judge us for those failures—may help us react less harshly toward those we see as acting sinfully in some way. And when we connect not only to our own brokenness, but also to the ways in which God has healed and restored us and renewed our hope, that empathy for others springs up even more readily. When we make these connections, we move beyond brokenness toward appreciation of and hopefulness for those we were once tempted to judge. We may become more conscious of our actions, and even of the words we use with each other—we may be more concretely loving with each other.

Years ago, while in college, my friends and I were out sharing our faith with anyone who would talk to us. We simply wanted to ask one question—"What do you think about Jesus?"—and see where that conversation took us. In one such conversation, a young woman said that she hated him. I asked why. She said because she could never love a god that killed her family. I asked her how she came to that conclusion, and she shared a story with me. When she was younger, her parents had allowed her to go to a sleepover at a friend's house. While she was away, the van that her parents and siblings were in was struck by another vehicle, and they were all killed in the accident. She was understandably devastated. When she went to the funeral, the clergy person presiding stated that this was God's will and that it was simply God's time to take them. What she heard in this message was that God had killed her parents. How could she love a god—how could she love Jesus—if Jesus had done this? My response was simple: God didn't cause the accident. God wept with you as you wept for your family. God loves you and God loves them. The young woman said it would be okay for us to pray for her. We prayed. After the prayer, she looked at us with tears in her eyes and simply said, "Thank you."

It seems that this young woman had not received compassion when she was most in need of it. And the same is true for so many people, in a number of different situations, whether they are trying to exit gang life or heal from the loss of a loved one.

The English word *compassion* can be broken down into two parts: "com" and "passion." We typically think of passion in terms of a strong emotion, but how then would we connect strong emotion and, say, the passion of Christ? Let's look at the deeper roots of the term. Our word *compassion* comes from the Latin roots *com* and *pati. Com* means "with" or "together" and *pati* means "to suffer." Centuries ago, *passion* had to do with the sufferings of Christ on the cross, and only later did it come to have the sense of strong emotion or desire. But even this strong emotion and desire stems from Jesus' suffering love for us on the cross, a love that itself was aimed at taking away our suffering. Matthew tells us,

> *Jesus traveled among all the cities and villages, teaching in their synagogues, announcing the good news of the kingdom, and healing every disease and every sickness. Now when Jesus saw the crowds, he had compassion for them because they were troubled and helpless, like sheep without a shepherd. Then he said to his disciples, "The size of the harvest is bigger than you can imagine, but there are few workers. Therefore, plead with the Lord of the harvest to send out workers for his harvest."*
>
> Matthew 9:35-38

And a little later on, in Matthew 10, Jesus gives the disciples authority and commissions them to go out on their own: "As you go, make this announcement: 'The kingdom of heaven has come near.' Heal the sick, raise the dead, cleanse those with skin diseases, and throw out demons" (Matthew 10:7-8).

Compassion can be the spark that gets the fire of transforming love going. In Exodus 2:23-24, when God hears the cries of the Israelites, God's response in sending Moses is one of compassion— God hears the suffering of the people. It is precisely this heart of compassion that Jesus came to show us. Jesus models a heart that constantly identifies with those he calls the least of these, the last and the lost of our world. This is how Jesus taught us to love one another.

Father Gregory Boyle offers a way of thinking about this compassionate move beyond judgment to love and gladness. In *Tattoos on the Heart*, Father Boyle talks about being in awe of what people carry instead of judging how they carry it.[1] Approaching others in awe of what they carry then helps us to love them into something new.

Let me give you an example. A teen mother who was part of our church ministry in Houston said she never thought she'd live past the age of twenty or so. Her life had been tough. She'd had a rough childhood and lived in a rough neighborhood. She'd made some poor decisions and figured that she might have three or four more years of life ahead of her if things continued to be this hard. This young woman said that she wanted to bring something good into this world before she left it, and so she had a child. In a way, she saw herself as giving birth to hope.

We are tempted to judge this young woman, to turn her into a cautionary tale, until we appreciate the context from which her thinking emerges. In darkness, she was seeking light, in the only way she knew how. Instead of running to condemn her, we can stand in awe of what she'd been through; we can stand in awe of the fact that she had any hope at all. We can look in awe at the fact that in the midst of a darkness that could easily have convinced her to give up, she trusted, in spite of every message about herself that she'd ever known, that she could bring something good into the world. And we can be thankful that she has turned to a loving

---

1   Gregory Boyle, *Tattoos on the Heart: The Power of Boundless Compassion* (New York: Free Press, 2010), 67.

community to help her make a good life, a new and hopeful life, for her and her child.

Now, living in awe of and thanksgiving for others doesn't, of course, mean that we proclaim that anything goes, and that any choice you want to make is a good or healthy one. But it does mean approaching every person, regardless of whether or not that person makes the best choices for the best of reasons, in love and compassion and support.

The fact unfortunately remains, though, that many people continue to be hurt by Christians who approach one another and the world in a spirit of judgment. I can only imagine that, as those who have been wounded by such judgment think about the Church, they are asking themselves, just like Tina Turner did, "What's love got to do with it?" They are asking the same questions that our culture at large asks about love, wondering, like the Black Eyed Peas did, "Where is the love?" If this is what the Church is, if this is what it does, what does love have to do with it at all?

LEARNING TO LIVE CHRIST'S LOVE

The Rev. Dr. Martin Luther King Jr. had a picture of the beloved community. At a 1957 conference on faith and race relations in Nashville, Tennessee, Dr. King said, "The end is the creation of the beloved community.... This type of love ... can transform opposers into friends.... It is the love of God working in the lives of men."[2]

---

2   Martin Luther King Jr., "The Role of the Church in Facing the Nation's Chief Moral Dilemma," speech, Conference on Christian Faith and Human Relations, April 25, 1957, Nashville, TN, transcript, http://okra.stanford .edu/transcription/document_images/Vol04Scans/184_1957_The %20Role%20of%20the%20Church.pdf.

Dr. King speaks about exactly what Carl found at Homeboy: the transformation of opposers—or enemies—into friends. This concept of transformative love is central to Christian life. But again, what does it mean? How does it transform us?

The transformative love that both Carl and Dr. King point to has two qualities. We might not speak very often about tenderness; this attitude or way of approaching others doesn't seem very popular in a culture that values strength and independence and self-sufficiency. In fact, it might feel downright risky to display this form of love that might be construed as weakness, especially when it's aimed at people in need of a second chance. If a politician suggested being tender with felons and repeat offenders, the accusations that would follow of being soft on crime would certainly destroy that politician's career.

Transformative love entails steadfastness, kindness, and mercy. It means sticking with each other, holding each other until we're whole. It means never giving up on ourselves or on each other.

But tenderness is precisely what we're called to display to each other in our love. And we can't just be tender once; the second aspect of transformative love entails steadfastness, kindness, and mercy. It means sticking with each other, holding each other until we're whole. It means never giving up on ourselves or on each other.

Well, this is all great, you'll say, but again, you're offering us a lot of nice-sounding words. Can you give us a picture of this tender, steadfast love?

While I was serving as a pastor in Houston, our church helped to launch a new nonprofit called Houston reVision. The organization was formed on the basis of feedback we'd received from the church about its needs and desires, and was inspired by the work of Father Gregory Boyle and Homeboy Industries. Now one of the city's growing nonprofits, which has brought in additional partners to share in its work, the initiative originally entailed a partnership between a United Methodist church and an Episcopal church, along with the support of the city's juvenile probation office and juvenile gang court.

I remember a student I came to know through reVision. I met this young man when he was in jail, where he'd landed after the crew he was riding around with got into an altercation that resulted in one person's death. This young man started out in the juvenile justice system, and was later moved into a facility for adults.

I began visiting him early in his time in jail. For a long time, he had no interest in me or my presence there; when I went to the prison, he stayed quiet, not really participating in the conversation.

But I kept at it, trying to extend some kindness to someone who had experienced very little of it, trying to be tender with a person who had known only hard realities. And eventually, that young man began to feel safe. He began to open up about his faith, about the need and desire for forgiveness. He even talked about the

Bible. As we kept talking, he started to dream, daring to imagine what he wanted his life to look like going forward.

Now, I won't lie and tell you that this young man has led a hugely successful or exemplary life outside of prison. In fact, he's still there. But he's also still reading his Bible—and is making use of what he finds in it. This person so many others had cast aside decided that he was going to live the best way he knew how. For as long as he remains in prison, he says that part of his ministry is to be a good witness to those who are around him. This young man has come to believe that you love people where you are, even if you don't love where you are.

BRINGING IT HOME: LOVE IN SCRIPTURE

As I think about that young man in Houston, I am reminded that loving the sin out of the world is what we observe most in the life of Jesus. Not only are we told this is the case in John 3:16—"God so loved the world that he gave his only Son, so that everyone who believes in him won't perish but will have eternal life"—but Jesus also demonstrated to us what love looks like. Jesus taught us how to love one another by loving us. His loving example was caught as much as it was taught, meaning that his disciples witnessed in him the kind of love that he preached.

The Apostle Paul reminds us what Jesus' demonstration of love looked like in Paul's letter to the Philippians. The third verse of the first chapter begins with thanksgiving. It begins with Paul reminding those he is addressing in the church of Philippi just how much they mean to him—he's reminding them that their souls have worth. Now, a thank-you does not give you your worth.

Your worth is already there. But a thank-you *does* serve to remind you of how much of a difference you make in the lives of those who have offered thanks.

After he gives thanks to the Philippians, in verse 9, Paul shifts his thoughts to prayer. The apostle's prayer is for love to be perfected. He writes them in the hopes that their "love might become even more and more rich with knowledge and all kinds of insight." It is a prayer for the growth of the beloved community—not just in terms of numbers, but also in terms of the depth of their transformative love for each other, their ability and commitment to be steadfast in their tender interaction with one another. It is growth into what we call "holiness" in my church tradition: the perfect love of God and neighbor. It is a prayer that expresses hope that the church in Philippi might be a place where we can set aside our felt need to hide our vulnerabilities and grow into a new holiness, a newly created family of love in which, as Carl and Dr. King said, enemies may be turned into friends.

And speaking of Carl, Homeboy has been a place that has even allowed him to be less of an enemy to himself. And able now to recognize the pain of his past life in a gang, he is able to live with the continuing repercussions of his personal history—wounds that include being unable to walk and being confined to a wheelchair—without allowing that past to define or limit him or his ability to love. "I really learned how to communicate my feelings. I learned how to love myself and I'm no longer living that selfish lifestyle that I once did. I come into these doors every day and I receive so much love. I wake up every day wanting to be here," he says.

You probably know someone like Carl, someone in need of tenderness, in need of the steadfast kindness that God offers us. My prayer is that we will learn the lessons of love that Christ is trying to teach us, and that this love—this tender, loving kindness—will be the law of our hearts and the guiding spirit behind all of our actions.

LOVE AND THE PRODIGAL

Jesus said, "A certain man had two sons. The younger son said to his father, 'Father, give me my share of the inheritance.' Then the father divided his estate between them. Soon afterward, the younger son gathered everything together and took a trip to a land far away. There, he wasted his wealth through extravagant living.

"When he had used up his resources, a severe food shortage arose in that country and he began to be in need. He hired himself out to one of the citizens of that country, who sent him into his fields to feed pigs. He longed to eat his fill from what the pigs ate, but no one gave him anything. When he came to his senses, he said, 'How many of my father's hired hands have more than enough food, but I'm starving to death! I will get up and go to my father, and say to him, "Father, I have sinned against heaven and against you. I no longer deserve to be called your son. Take me on as one of your hired hands."' So he got up and went to his father.

"While he was still a long way off, his father saw him and was moved with compassion. His father ran to

him, hugged him, and kissed him. Then his son said, 'Father, I have sinned against heaven and against you. I no longer deserve to be called your son.' But the father said to his servants, 'Quickly, bring out the best robe and put it on him! Put a ring on his finger and sandals on his feet! Fetch the fattened calf and slaughter it. We must celebrate with feasting because this son of mine was dead and has come back to life! He was lost and is found!' And they began to celebrate.

"Now his older son was in the field. Coming in from the field, he approached the house and heard music and dancing. He called one of the servants and asked what was going on. The servant replied, 'Your brother has arrived, and your father has slaughtered the fattened calf because he received his son back safe and sound.' Then the older son was furious and didn't want to enter in, but his father came out and begged him. He answered his father, 'Look, I've served you all these years, and I never disobeyed your instruction. Yet you've never given me as much as a young goat so I could celebrate with my friends. But when this son of yours returned, after gobbling up your estate on prostitutes, you slaughtered the fattened calf for him.' Then his father said, 'Son, you are always with me, and everything I have is yours. But we had to celebrate and be glad because this brother of yours was dead and is alive. He was lost and is found.'"

Luke 15:11-32

I'm sure you know the story of the prodigal son. It's been told so many times, we even hear people in the wider culture refer to problem children as prodigal sons or daughters—seen maybe as troublemakers who just don't learn, whose wild wanderings bring nothing but fear and helplessness, and sometimes even resentment, to those who love them and who try in futile fashion to protect them or instill some sort of sense of basic responsibility into them.

I imagine it being much the same with the family mentioned in Luke. A father realizing his son just can't be governed by the same desires or motivations as the rest of the community, that he's going to do his own thing, whether or not the father tries to stop him. And so the father lets his child make his own mistakes, maybe hoping the young man will be able to find some place he can fit in and settle down—to "find himself," as we might say today. Even if no one else understands him, maybe if he lets his son go his own way, his child will finally find some peace.

And in the meantime, the father's older boy does everything right: he obeys his father; he obeys his wishes that his son continue the family business; he gets along with everyone around him and is responsible and helpful. Maybe he's so responsible and helpful by nature, everyone takes for granted that this is just who he is; that he has the life he's always hoped for. And maybe when his younger brother decides to leave, this older one thinks it is for the best; he has seen how his little brother was hurting his father, how he was causing trouble for everyone, with all his restlessness and need to see the world. And so the younger son leaves, and things are fine; things finally run smoothly. The crops are growing; the workers are happy. His father is worried about what has become of his younger son, but really, the older brother thinks, that would always be the case, no matter where his frustrating brother was.

And then this wasteful black sheep just shows back up. After losing everything through no one's fault but his own and probably not working a day since he left his father's house, the young man shows up and expects everyone to be happy about it. Sure, he sounds apologetic, but did he think about how much he hurt everyone in the household, how much of his work they have all had to assume thanks to his dropping his share? The older brother has been working hard since his younger brother went away; in fact, he's been working hard all his life, and that's just what everyone has always expected. And so, to come home and find dancing and music, and everyone in an uproar, when this responsible older brother has never even been allowed to have a barbecue with his friends and relax—and then to find the cause of all this rejoicing is because his useless brother has come home begging for forgiveness? Well, it could be just a little much to handle. What about his own dreams, this hardworking older brother? He's had to dismiss them just like almost everyone else has, and now, not only does his younger brother get to go and do just as he pleases, and with their father's money to boot, but he also gets to come back and be coddled and celebrated, without so much as a frown or one of those classic lectures their father could give. With all of that going on, you might understand why this older brother isn't all that eager to join in the celebration.

But look at the father, look at his reasoning, and think about what we've been saying about God's love. Maybe the father was angry; I'm sure he certainly disapproved of what his son had been doing. But ask most parents, and they'll tell you that no matter how mad they get with their kids, if they don't know where they are, if they don't know whether they're safe—whatever their kids have done, they're worried sick about them. They worry about them all the time, in fact—because the essential fact about the way they relate to them is that they love them, and no matter how many second chances they've used up and wasted, parents would do anything to make sure their kids are safe, and are part of their lives.

So imagine how much grief and worry this father was going through before his younger son came back home. Had he done something wrong, something to drive his son away? Had he raised him wrong? What if he'd been hurt, or worse, and it was the father's fault for letting him go in the first place? What if his son never realized how much his father loved him? All of this and more must have been going through the father's head. To see his son walking up the road—to see him alive, and coming back to him—all of the lectures and the worry must have fallen away. All of the disappointments, all of the justifications he knew he might have to make to family and friends, were gone. Because the most basic reality about the father and his son was that the father loved his child. The father saw a second chance for all of them: for his younger son, who was safe and had come home and had a second chance at life; for his relationships with both of his boys, whom he probably knew now he could never take for granted; for the relationship between brothers, which had a chance now to be healed and find its way forward.

Love that has to deal with tough situations like these isn't an easy one to maintain. Indeed, I think we often assume love means everything's going to be easy: that we won't argue or get irritated with each other; that we'll always want to be around each other; and that disagreements will be smoothed over in the midst of love that will solve everything.

Love is patient—love sticks with the beloved, even when that beloved person doesn't seem very likable at all.

That might be nice. But as we've been talking about, love is patient—love sticks with the beloved, even when that beloved person doesn't seem very likable at all. Love will do the hard, steadfast work to see past the dislike of the now, and gain its strength from the love that transcends the moments and the hurts that can so easily add up if we lose sight of who we're called to be.

Maybe the family in Luke never healed; maybe the older brother never could get over his resentment with the way his younger sibling acted and was treated. But I have an idea that the love this father showed his wayward child was so radical— so beyond reason and obviously grounded in something greater than rules and right behavior—that its strength and power of forgiveness spread to everyone around. That healing ensued.

If this is what God's love looks like, how could we fail to extend it to others? How could we fail to hope that all of those prodigals in our lives will return to us, and how could we do anything but open our arms to them in thanksgiving and joy?

DEVOTION

One of the most fundamental human emotions is love. Love is one of the first emotions we should feel from others and one of the first that we should learn to express. From our earliest moments in life, we are meant to learn the warmth and care of people who love us.

We know, however, that not every person is surrounded by a community of love from birth. Not everyone is surrounded by communities of love as they grow older. Love is God's intent for us, but sometimes the communities and relationships we form do not express the best of God's intention. Even still, as we look at music, poems, plays, movies, musicals, visual art, dance, and literature, we find that love is everywhere. We play love and images of love all around us almost as if to remind us of what is most important.

We love because, according to 1 John 4:8, "God is love." We always create out of who we are, and so this God who is love created us in a spirit of love to be loving. All over Scripture, we find encouragement to love. In John 13:34, when Jesus gives a new commandment to his disciples he simply says, "Love each other."

This love that we were created by and for is active. God calls us to the active work of loving one another and loving this world. There are so many people out there who struggle to feel their worth because they have not been shown genuine love from others. When we don't feel loved, we close ourselves off. We build walls to keep others out so that we won't be hurt again. As we numb ourselves to the hurts of the world, we can easily cause hurt along the way to ourselves and others. Love acts as a restorative balm to heal that which is wounded and to make whole.

It is amazing what love and tenderness can do to breathe new life into a person and into situations. Allow God's love to fill every corner of your life and allow it to flow out of your life into the lives of others. There are so many people who are looking for the no-strings-attached agape love that God calls the people of God to—a love that doesn't have pre-conditions and a love that does not discriminate. Let this kind of love be your guide and bless the world.

God of love, we pray that you would restore our hearts of love toward one another and that our restored hearts would transform the world. Amen.

Chapter 3

Your Joy Will Be Complete

Chapter 3

YOUR JOY WILL
BE COMPLETE

Rejoice, Daughter Zion! Shout, Israel!
Rejoice and exult with all your heart, Daughter
Jerusalem.
The LORD has removed your judgment;
he has turned away your enemy.
The LORD, the king of Israel, is in your midst;
you will no longer fear evil.
On that day, it will be said to Jerusalem:
Don't fear, Zion.
Don't let your hands fall.
The LORD your God is in your midst—a warrior
bringing victory.
He will create calm with his love;
he will rejoice over you with singing.

I will remove from you those worried about the
appointed feasts.
They have been a burden for her, a reproach.
Watch what I am about to do to all your oppressors
at that time.
  I will deliver the lame;
  I will gather the outcast.
  I will change their shame into praise and fame
  throughout the earth.
At that time, I will bring all of you back,
  at the time when I gather you.
  I will give you fame and praise among all the
  neighboring peoples
      when I restore your possessions and you can
      see them—says the LORD.

Zephaniah 3:14-20

THEO: THE JOY OF RECONCILIATION

Before he got involved with Homeboy Industries, Theo felt
trapped in a negative environment. Using drugs, spending most of
his time in the street with gang members, he says he was "heartbroken." But as Father Gregory Boyle and the staff at Homeboy
began offering him support and assistance, Theo says he began
"opening up his eyes." He was astounded that people from outside his neighborhood were willing not only to welcome and help
him but also to provide more support than any people he'd known
before. In this place where the doors are never closed to anyone,
Theo experiences "a feeling of joy" being around onetime enemies
who now "are just a single family"—who, he says, "look out for one
another."

The Joy of Christ

Let's look again at the hymn "O Holy Night." In verse one, we're told that "the weary world rejoices" at the birth of Christ. What's central to rejoicing? Well—joy.

It seems like such a simple word, *joy*. We might be tempted to read those three letters as if they formed a synonym for happiness, or could be used to point to a particularly good mood. But those interpretations don't quite get at the particular nature, at the fullness, of the emotion we're seeing in this verse.

It turns out that the concept of joy has a whole history in the Scriptures, and is, of course, deeply connected to God and God's very nature. Often, it seems that Scripture is telling us that joy is something God has, something that we need to be given. For example, joy is mentioned in Ecclesiastes 5:18-20 as something that is given to humankind by God as a gift:

> *This is the one good thing I've seen: it's appropriate*
> *for people to eat, drink, and find enjoyment in all*
> *their hard work under the sun during the brief*
> *lifetime that God gives them because that's their*
> *lot in life. Also, whenever God gives people wealth*
> *and riches and enables them to enjoy it, to accept*
> *their place in the world and to find pleasure in*
> *their hard work—all this is God's gift. Indeed,*
> *people shouldn't brood too much over the days*
> *of their lives because God gives an answer in their*
> *hearts' joy.*
>
> *Ecclesiastes 5:18-20*

Is it the case that, made as we are in God's image, we all have the same capacity for joy? Let's look more closely at what the Bible has to say about the concept.

Verse seventeen of Zephaniah 3 says that God rejoices over us. In English, that might seem clear enough. But biblical Hebrew has many different words we could translate as "rejoice."

One is *gila*. When I tell you that this term is related to the word for wave, *gal*, it should come as no surprise that even though *gila* signals a strong or intense sensation of joy, this emotion or experience is very short-lived, abandoning a person almost as soon as it appears. This fleeting sense of joy does indeed come over us as a wave, and is gone just as quickly as ocean waters rise and fall.

So *gila* isn't quite what we're getting at. Let's look at a couple of other Hebrew words related to joy: *rina* and *ditza*. Both of these terms convey a sense or experience of elation, but each is exercised in a unique physical way. *Rina* is manifested in singing or shouting, while *ditza* is related to dancing. These terms convey a sense of excitement that can't be kept quiet, that has to be announced in some way, whether vocally or visually. Joy expressed as *rina* or *ditza* does seem irrepressible—but like *gila*, the emotion described with these terms lasts only as long as the activity that makes it known.

I always think about this form of joy and its impermanence when I read the story of David bringing the Ark of the Covenant into Jerusalem. Only recently having consolidated his position as king of Israel, David wants to make Jerusalem into the kingdom's most holy city, and he thinks a nice way to get that process off the ground is to bring what is considered God's house into the city:

Once again David assembled the select warriors
of Israel, thirty thousand strong. David and all the
troops who were with him set out for Baalah, which
is Kiriath-jearim of Judah, to bring God's chest up
from there—the chest that is called by the name of
the LORD of heavenly forces, who sits enthroned on
the winged creatures. They loaded God's chest on
a new cart and carried it from Abinadab's house,
which was on the hill. Uzzah and Ahio, Abinadab's
sons, were driving the new cart. Uzzah was beside
God's chest while Ahio was walking in front of it.
Meanwhile, David and the entire house of Israel
celebrated in the LORD's presence with all their
strength, with songs, zithers, harps, tambourines,
rattles, and cymbals.

When they approached Nacon's threshing floor,
Uzzah reached out to God's chest and grabbed it
because the oxen had stumbled. The LORD became
angry at Uzzah, and God struck him there because
of his mistake, and he died there next to God's chest.
Then David got angry because the LORD's anger
lashed out against Uzzah, and so that place is called
Perez-uzzah today.

2 Samuel 6:1-8

Notice how David's joy and triumph—grounded in his belief
that his plans are right—so quickly turns to anger. Even though
he believes he's doing everything for the glory of God, his joyful
celebration is really grounded in something else—his own pride.

And as soon as that pride gets shown up for what it is when it's made clear that God has *other* plans for a dwelling place, David's joy evaporates.

> *The desert and the dry land will be glad;*
> > *the wilderness will rejoice and blossom like*
> > *the crocus.*
> *They will burst into bloom,*
> > *and rejoice with joy and singing.*
> *They will receive the glory of Lebanon,*
> > *the splendor of Carmel and Sharon.*
> *They will see the LORD's glory,*
> > *the splendor of our God.*
>
> *Strengthen the weak hands,*
> > *and support the unsteady knees.*
> *Say to those who are panicking:*
> > *"Be strong! Don't fear!*
> > *Here's your God,*
> > > *coming with vengeance;*
> > > *with divine retribution*
> > *God will come to save you."*
>
> *Then the eyes of the blind will be opened,*
> > *and the ears of the deaf will be cleared.*
> *Then the lame will leap like the deer,*
> > *and the tongue of the speechless will sing.*
> *Waters will spring up in the desert,*
> > *and streams in the wilderness.*
> *The burning sand will become a pool,*
> > *and the thirsty ground, fountains of water.*

The jackals' habitat, a pasture;
grass will become reeds and rushes.
A highway will be there.
It will be called The Holy Way.
The unclean won't travel on it,
but it will be for those walking on that way.
Even fools won't get lost on it;
no lion will be there,
and no predator will go up on it.
None of these will be there;
only the redeemed will walk on it.
The Lord's ransomed ones will return and enter
Zion with singing,
with everlasting joy upon their heads.
Happiness and joy will overwhelm them;
grief and groaning will flee away.

Isaiah 35:1-10

Remember we talked about the hope Jeremiah offered the exiles in Babylon? It turns out he knew what he was talking about—not just because of what really did happen to the exiles after Cyrus came into power, but also because he knew what had happened to the Jewish people in the past. We might say today that his historical consciousness gave him the knowledge and the tools to know how to address these types of situations.

A little more than a century before the Babylonians destroyed the Temple in Jerusalem and sent the kingdom's leaders into exile, the Assyrians were the reigning power in the region—and unsurprisingly, not everyone was happy with the situation. Not long before Isaiah wrote the passage quoted above, Judah's king,

Hezekiah, briefly took part in a multinational revolt against the rulers—one of many rumblings that finally led to the Assyrians placing Jerusalem under siege.

Isaiah had been warning the king and leaders for a while that they were essentially digging their own graves; that their behavior was hardly worthy of God's people, and they would suffer accordingly unless they changed their ways. But in chapter 35, Isaiah seems to take a different tack, and gives his addressees a picture of what right relationship, of what faith and God-centered hope and action, will look like. The prophet is giving his readers a picture of assurance-filled joy, based on the knowledge that God is with them.

Indeed, not that long after the Assyrians surrounded Jerusalem, a curious thing happened. Normally ruthless with their enemies, one day the Assyrians just put an end to the siege; they just got up and left. Maybe they decided that their resources would be better used elsewhere; maybe they thought teaching such a small city-state a lesson just wasn't worth it, especially if it could contribute resources to the empire instead of being wiped out. Maybe they thought a good scare would be enough to make Jerusalem get back into line and pay its tribute.

Whatever the case, there must have been great rejoicing to see the enemies heading back to where they'd come from. Even though the world in which they lived was filled with warring factions and violent power grabs, even though they knew that peace on the ground was often just a matter of lucky circumstance, they had been shown what they must have believed was God's direct intervention in their lives. Enemies known to be needlessly violent, notoriously vicious, just letting easy prey go unscathed? Unheard of! Something so incredibly strange could only come from God—could only be a gift no attacker would choose to grant on his own. Something beyond human comprehension—something beyond the normal law of cause and effect, of circumstances, had to be happening here.

Indeed, there was joy to be had at what was much more than a lucky escape—and relief-filled joy like none they'd ever known. On the Holy Way Isaiah describes, in the world Isaiah describes, where nature doesn't act like any natural world that we're familiar with, problems will pop up again down the road—but the people on God's Holy Way will also know overwhelming, maybe even baffling, joy. Because they are God's people, and because that is the way of God.

We've dismissed three different types of joy as inadequate to the joy God takes in us. What about the word *hanaah*—does this term get us any closer to the concept Zephaniah uses in telling us that God rejoices over us? Well, I hate to tell you that it doesn't; *hanaah* conveys a sense of joy in or enjoyment of something very specific, something that can't be applied to an all-encompassing, or even general, sense of delight.

So, we've tossed out all of these different ways of experiencing or showing joy. Which word *does* Zephaniah use when he talks about God's joy in us, his creatures? In verse three, the prophet uses the word *simcha*, a term that denotes whole—complete—happiness or contentment.

Simcha can be a verb, as it is in Zephaniah 3, or it can be a noun. Because of this grammatical flexibility, we can describe Christmas—the celebration of the birth of Christ and anticipation of the second coming of Christ—as *simcha*. But this term isn't meant to be used exclusively for divine matters; the birth of a child can be described using *simcha*, as could a gathering of family or friends during a holiday.

So we know that God experiences complete happiness in us. And as I just mentioned, humans, too, can experience this same emotion. So it makes sense that in Ecclesiastes, joy is mentioned as something that is given to humankind by God as a gift. In the Gospel of John, Jesus points to this divine gift to humans, instructing his disciples so that his joy will be complete in them.

Consider Jesus' words as recorded in John:

> *"As the Father loved me, I too have loved you.*
> *Remain in my love. If you keep my commandments,*
> *you will remain in my love, just as I kept my Father's*
> *commandments and remain in his love. I have said*
> *these things to you so that my joy will be in you and*
> *your joy will be complete."*
>
> John 15:9-11

What does it mean for God's joy—God's *simcha* or complete joy—to become complete in us?

LEARNING TO LIVE CHRIST'S JOY

I've mentioned some events—the birth of a child or a family gathering—that could exemplify *simcha*. But do we have a way of thinking about this concept in our own language? In English, the word *rejoice*, in its more original or archaic sense, meant "to cause to joy." In a modern sense, we talk about the ability "to feel or show joy or delight."

When we rejoice over one another—when we delight in one another—we are, in a sense, offering the joy we have to the other person.

I love the old sense of the word. It reminds us that joy is something that can be transferred. When we rejoice over one another—when we delight in one another—we are, in a sense, offering the joy we have to the other person. We are re-joy-ing. We are regifting a joy that was given to us. And this gifting and regifting of joy never diminishes the quality of the joy.

As you might have guessed, this joy has a lot to do with love. I talked in the last chapter about loving sin out of the world instead of trying to eradicate it through judgment—through what we might want to call the removal of joy. Let's bring that steadfast, tender love back into the picture and look at how regifting the joy we've been given is often shown by giving—gifting—a second chance to people.

I also spoke in the last chapter about the reVision initiative in Houston. In our work there with juvenile gang members and other teens who were living on life's margins, we became familiar with a research-based framework called 40 Developmental Assets. This report lays out the forty essential assets children require for a healthy life—assets such as family support, safety, high expectations, and the power to resist peer pressure. The version of the framework we use is primarily focused on youth between the ages of twelve and eighteen.

What the 40 Developmental Assets tells us is that the more assets youth have as they develop, the greater their chances will be to lead productive and responsible lives. With fewer assets to rely on as they develop, young people are more likely to engage in impulsive or dangerous behaviors such as addiction, violence, and unhealthy relationships—behaviors whose likelihood decreases as the number of assets they enjoy increases.

As Father Boyle puts it, the youth sought out by reVision were experiencing a "lethal absence of hope."[1] Given their childhoods, their past histories, and the environments in which they were living, it makes sense—and it makes sense, too, that this lack of hope brought on by the tough realities they knew also led to a lack of joy. Think about it: have you ever had something that you treasured, but were afraid to lose? This fear—a strange one—is a kind of loss aversion. We enjoy something, we fear losing it, and ultimately we fear feeling the absence of what we treasured. Joy is something that we are sometimes afraid to lose. Complete joy is a treasure that many of us desire in various areas of our lives, but accompanying that desire for joy can also be the anticipation of its loss.

My friend and colleague the Rev. Laura Isaac shared with our church a powerful story about joy and fear of loss. She said:

> About a week into our daughter's life, I sat on our couch

---

1   Gregory Boyle, *Barking to the Choir: The Power of Radical Kinship* (New York: Simon & Schuster, 2017), 130–131.

admiring every wrinkle and feature of her sweet face as she slept in my arms. I remember going through this cycle of emotions as I sat there gazing at her. At first, I was overcome with joy. And then a bit of a panic. And then gratitude. And then panic again. And then turned to my husband and with tears in my eyes and a lump in my throat said, "Oh, Logan, she's so beautiful even if she died tomorrow I'd be so thankful to have gotten to be her mom for this week." I couldn't bear to move into the place of vulnerability that so graciously hosted my joy in that moment. I needed to protect my heart that no longer felt like it was in my own body, but cradled in my arms. This act of foreboding joy by practicing tragedy does not actually bring God's peace even though it feels like guarding our hearts and minds.

So many of the dysfunctions and addictions that we face in our society are due to ways we seek to numb or take the edge off of what we are feeling. We seek to take the edge off of pain through things that bring us instant comfort or gratification. We take the edge off of joy by dwelling on former or potential pain or loss. We take the edge off of our boredom by various kinds of entertainment, sometimes dangerous and unhealthy ones. And if your daily life contains very little that isn't painful, the ability to believe you can find—much less maintain—any joy is probably very low. Instead of basking in the joy you find, you'll protect yourself from getting hurt by its loss.

Theo from Homeboy says, "When I first came to Homeboy... I was on the street, I was using drugs, and I was heartbroken." When your heart has been broken too often, you often begin to anticipate continued brokenness and to do what you can to protect yourself against continued pain. In Houston, at reVision, I would often encounter young people who smoked cannabis from time to time. Rarely did I meet students who had problems with underage drinking, because they had seen that form of addiction cause too much destruction in the lives of people around them. Why all the smoking, though? Well, when life is so regularly painful, people do what they can to compensate—to take the edge off of the experience. The fear they experience is actually fear of feeling— feeling the pain or even feeling the joy because the loss of joy is painful.

Joy is not the same as happiness. Joy is not a feeling to be conjured up that then remains vulnerable to being taken away in a moment; joy is an assurance.

The possibility of having joy, then, is hard for some of us to open ourselves up to until we realize that joy is not the same as happiness. Joy is not a feeling to be conjured up that then remains vulnerable to being taken away in a moment; joy is an assurance.

Think about the hymn "Blessed Assurance":

> Blessed assurance, Jesus is mine!
> O what a foretaste of glory divine!
> Heir of salvation, purchase of God,
> born of his Spirit, washed in his blood.

There is something unique about knowing that you are in Christ. That Christ is in your heart. That Christ is your savior, and that in that way, Christ is yours. It's assurance. Assurance is a confidence in what you have. "Blessed Assurance" has always seemed a joyful hymn to me because the joy comes from assurance in Christ. Here we see that joy is something that we have because it has been given.

But what can we do for people who have no assurance—who, like participants taking that first step into Homeboy or reVision, are also experiencing a lethal absence of *simcha* joy and of healthy relationship—who are suffering from a lethal absence of the church?

Both Homeboy and reVision are ministries of presence, of providing the steadfast, tender love and kindness needed to allow *simcha* to take root. Those are good aims, goals that we want to achieve for kids in need. But in Houston, it was also amazing to realize that once these young people became involved with the program, it wasn't just us giving joy to these troubled youth in a one-directional transaction; through reVision's ministry, both the young people and the staff working with them found joy in each other. Mentors and mentees learned to rejoice over one another just as God rejoices over us. I loved watching our eldest volunteer, Louis, interact with the young people who were part of reVision. Louis was around ninety years old, and he would share World War II stories and pictures with the youth. They would just eat these stories up. They would laugh together and talk about life. To watch Louis and these young people was to witness moments of mutuality where every soul felt its own and each other's worth, and rejoiced.

This mutuality was especially evident during the community meals we held for reVision youth and volunteers. Our staff would bring the youth together once a week, and volunteers from church would help the young people prepare the food. I remember that one of the early meals we cooked together was homemade pizza. We laughed, told stories, cut up ingredients, and just plain cut up together. Each young person created his or her own take on the pizza theme, and we treated each creation as special. In this new home we had created, we delighted in what we'd made and we delighted in one another. We delighted in the safe space we'd been given, and in the way it allowed us to, as Theo said, open our eyes to each other and look out for each other. We transferred our joy back and forth between each other—we rejoiced.

The mutual joy I witnessed at reVision is so similar to what I see with my three boys. Each of them is fun and unique. I love laughing with them now, but I really got a kick out of laughing and smiling with them when they were babies. Babies' vision takes a while to develop. At first, they can see clearly only within a few inches. This is, in part, why we are so attached to faces and expressions. The way we first learn about the world takes place in the distance between the arms and the face of a caring adult. In that first home, in the space of between six and ten inches, we learn laughter and crying, joy and sadness, confusion and clarity, fear and comfort, all by watching that face above us as we are held in the arms that surround us. Babies learn by mirroring the expressions that they see. What we pour over them becomes their first learning.

At such a young age, children are sponges, absorbing what you share with them and then sharing it back with you and the world.

You smile, they smile. You laugh, they laugh. You pour joy over them and then they mirror that joy. The mirroring of joy that a baby displays is an act of re-joy-ing. The joy that is shared with them is then shared back with the world. I cannot help believing this is part of God's intention. In the sweet interactions between parent and child, formation begins—in a way, discipleship begins. In the sharing of the expressions on a face, we begin to learn how to face the world. I'm no developmental psychologist, but I cannot imagine that it hurts to share a lot of authentic joy with a child and then watch that child share joy with the world.

If we want to see transformation in the life of the world, we must stop closing ourselves off to those who would benefit from such transformation.

I don't think we ever really lose what we first learned. We learn to be selective about what we do or do not receive into our lives, but we still act as sponges. We take things in and then we pour things out into the world. I continue to think about Theo's story. He experienced joy being poured into his life day after day in the interactions and care that he received at Homeboy Industries. Theo shared with me that the lives of many of those who come to Homeboy had previously been filled with "negative stuff." All kinds of pain and all kinds of absence, but Homeboy opens the floodgates and pours love in. This, I think, is the calling of all Christian community. If we want to see transformation in the life of the world, we must stop closing ourselves off to those who would benefit from such transformation. The witness of Homeboy is that enemies become friends in this kind of dynamic.

BRINGING IT HOME: JOY IN SCRIPTURE

Be glad in the Lord always! Again I say, be glad!
Let your gentleness show in your treatment of all
people. The Lord is near. Don't be anxious about
anything; rather, bring up all of your requests to
God in your prayers and petitions, along with
giving thanks. Then the peace of God that exceeds
all understanding will keep your hearts and minds
safe in Christ Jesus.

Philippians 4:4-7

Let's go back one more time to Theo. He wasn't only summing up his roots in Los Angeles; he could also have been talking about reVision's youth in Houston when he said, "The background we came from is nothing but negative stuff." Little to no resources, little to no hope of anyone trusting these young people or helping them or being thankful for their presence. But in Los Angeles and beyond, Homeboy has given participants the ability not to "be anxious about anything," because they've found the joy of kinship, of knowing that they're supported, of experiencing "the peace of God that will keep their hearts and minds safe in Christ Jesus."

They've found the joy of kinship.

And the joy isn't just in being safe and loved; Father Gregory Boyle says that this joy is rooted in what he calls "being in companionship with Jesus." This companionship is summed up by St. Ignatius's call to "see Jesus standing in the lowly place." Boyle says that when he himself stands in that lowly place with Jesus, "with the easily despised and the readily left out, and with the demonized so that the demonizing will stop, and with the disposable so that the day will come when we stop throwing people away...I find the fullness of life."[2] He finds joy not in being safe himself—but in standing with others who dwell on the margins, in the midst of danger and hopelessness. He finds joy in carrying out the call found in Philippians to "Let your gentleness show in your treatment of all people."

As we await the coming of Christ, the one born in a lowly place to serve those living in a lowly place, let us open ourselves to the joys of supporting each other, of trusting each other—to the joys of living together in the kinship that Christ offers. As we learn to live into this new life, we can remember the Celtic blessing that speaks to the kind of joy that I hope is experienced by all who have encountered Christ and the kindred community of joy that Christ calls us to.

---

2   Gregory Boyle, "The Calling of Delight: Gangs, Service, and Kinship," interview by Krista Tippett, *On Being*, The On Being Project, April 2, 2015, audio, 50:59, https://onbeing.org/programs/greg-boyle-the-calling-of -delight-gangs-service-and-kinship/.

Blessing

> May the peace of the Lord Christ go with you,
> wherever He may send you.
> May He guide you through the wilderness,
> protect you through the storm.
> May He bring you home rejoicing
> at the wonders He has shown you.
> May He bring you home rejoicing
> once again into our doors.[3]

3   Northumbria Community, *Celtic Daily Prayer* (San Francisco, HarperSanFrancisco, 2002), 19, http://www.worldcat.org/title/celtic-daily -prayer-from-the-northumbria-community/oclc/49389377/viewport.

DEVOTION

Every now and then, I meet a person who is truly joyful. Joy just exudes from their person in such a contagious way that you can't quite help being joyful with them. Think of someone like this in your own life. People like this bring laughter and joy to every occasion with their smiles, their good cheer, their optimism, and their care for you. This kind of joy spills over and even if you are having a sour day, it becomes hard not to smile just a little when this joy is shared, and then we begin to rejoice. It is a re-gifting of joy or a re-joy-ing.

Scripture encourages us to rejoice. First Thessalonians 5:16-18 puts it this way: "Rejoice always. Pray continually. Give thanks in every situation because this is God's will for you in Christ Jesus."

"Rejoice always." This is a wonderful bit of spiritual direction, but *always*? Can we really rejoice always? Some days it is easier to rejoice than others. Some days things seem to be going our way. We are happy in our relationships, fulfilled by the meaningful work that we are doing in our workplaces, and generally thriving. Other days we feel a bit more fragile. Sometimes life does not seem to be going our way and we experience frustration in areas of our lives. How can we rejoice in challenging times?

I find that giving thanks helps to keep one's heart centered on the joy of the Lord. The most joyful people that I have known are those who can give thanks and praise God in the midst of every situation. Giving thanks reminds us of the blessings that we receive from God each and every day and are a reminder of the love and provision that we daily receive from God. There is always something good in the world to be celebrated. Even in the midst of hardship we learn to say, "I'm gonna praise him anyhow!"

As we practice rejoicing, may we become people who rejoice. May the spirit of rejoicing in Christ wash away our weariness and may we begin to so rejoice over others that their weariness will turn into rejoicing because of what God has done for us in Christ Jesus.

O God who rejoices over us, help us to rejoice in you and your truth. Help us to rejoice in the lives of others and may our joy be a gift that we bring to the world. Amen.

Chapter 4

CHRIST IS OUR PEACE

Chapter 4

CHRIST IS OUR PEACE

As for you, Bethlehem of Ephrathah,
though you are the least significant of Judah's forces,
one who is to be a ruler in Israel on my
behalf will come out from you.
His origin is from remote times, from ancient days.
Therefore, he will give them up
until the time when she who is in labor gives birth.
The rest of his kin will return to the people of Israel.
He will stand and shepherd his flock in the strength
of the LORD,
in the majesty of the name of the LORD his God.
They will dwell secure,
because he will surely become great throughout
the earth;
he will become one of peace.

Micah 5:2-5a

Mary said,

"With all my heart I glorify the Lord!
    In the depths of who I am I rejoice in God
    my savior.
He has looked with favor on the low status of his
servant.
    Look! From now on, everyone will consider
    me highly favored
        because the mighty one has done great
        things for me.
Holy is his name.
    He shows mercy to everyone,
        from one generation to the next,
        who honors him as God.
He has shown strength with his arm.
    He has scattered those with arrogant
    thoughts and proud inclinations.
    He has pulled the powerful down from their
    thrones
        and lifted up the lowly.
He has filled the hungry with good things
    and sent the rich away empty-handed.
He has come to the aid of his servant Israel,
    remembering his mercy,
    just as he promised to our ancestors,
        to Abraham and to Abraham's
        descendants forever."

Luke 1:46-55

CHRISTINA: THE PEACE OF FAMILY

Before Christina came to Homeboy Industries, she was having a hard time on her own—with the big things, like getting sober and finishing school, and even with the things that should have been easy, like spending time with her daughter. But Homeboy has been helping to make things less stressful for her, providing Christina with tools to help her focus, to form relationships, to live the life she wants to live. One of the things she values about the therapy sessions and the classes Homeboy offers her is the fact that, as she says, "everyone is going through the exact same thing you are going through. It feels so good to have that support." She credits the organization with helping her work toward her high school diploma, and toward becoming a drug and alcohol counselor. And even more importantly, Homeboy has given her the peace "to be present" with her daughter. Because of this loving home of strangers who have become a family, Christina has also found the peace that has enabled her to make a new, loving home with the family she's always had.

THE PEACE OF CHRIST

Remember "O Holy Night"? Believe it or not, that hymn still has more to offer us in terms of helping us think about what Advent means for our lives. This week we focus on one of its verses that says:

> Truly he taught us to love one another;
> His law is love and his gospel is peace.
> Chains shall he break, for the slave is our brother,
> And in his name all oppression shall cease.

So, Christ's gospel—the good news Christ has to offer us—is peace. We think of Christmas as a time of peace, and we also say it throughout the year: "The peace of Christ be with you." But what is this peace? The word gets used in so many contexts and for so many purposes, both within and outside of the church, we may not even stop and think anymore about what it really means.

Turn on the news on any given day, and you'll probably hear a story involving peace, or the absence of it, or various attempts to achieve or maintain it. Chances are, these stories involve the world of what could generally be called politics: treaties and elected officials, world leaders and diplomats, and warring factions trying to decide how to get along (or not) with everyone walking away satisfied.

What are these parties trying to accomplish? What do they mean when they say they're working for peace?

The absence of physical conflict is probably the most basic way of thinking about peace, and this is the sense that's most prevalent in political discussions of the idea. Whether that means the absence of war or of gang violence or a life free of domestic abuse, peace at its simplest level may just point to the assurance of existing without having to fear physical harm.

But of course, peace means much more than that; we need more than a very basic level of physical safety to have a full life. If peace is the freedom from being harassed in a physical way, it also has the sense of being free from other sorts of threats, and from the stress and worry that come along with them. For so many people trying to make ends meet, those stresses are financial; worrying about how to pay the rent or a hospital bill may take up so much physical and mental energy, there's no way we can say such an existence is peaceful. And the worries that lie beneath those financial burdens—whether I'll have a roof over my head, whether I'll be able to have an operation I desperately need but can't pay for—add entirely new barriers to achieving the calm and assurance that come along with a peaceful life. Even less weighty stressors, such as a hectic workplace or a chaotic household, block our ability to believe that peace is attainable.

It's understandable that we try to eliminate all these forms of stressful living—and indeed, we need to find healthy, constructive ways to deal with them if we're to have productive and happy lives. But even when we do succeed in something as small as defusing a tense situation at the office or something as monumental as achieving a ceasefire between enemy factions, we know that the fears and weighty emotions behind them will never go away completely, and that some new storm will pop up again somewhere else all too soon. When you solve a problem in one area, another will crop up. Leaders will come and go, treaties will be dissolved, and laws will be changed. New coworkers will appear and homes will age and have to be repaired. That vacation that lets you get away from it all is over almost as soon as it begins. Even the peace of a Christmas Eve service, with the candles glowing and thoughts of rest and family and celebration, will probably give way to the chaos that often comes along with the holiday season. Peace that aims at and achieves the elimination of these types of worries is circumstantial. This type of peace comes and goes. It never lasts.

If circumstantial peace comes and goes, that can't be what Christ is offering us, can it? If what we receive from Christ were only a temporary peace, what difference would that make? Surely what he offers us is a peace that is rooted in something deeper.

Let's take a step back and look at where we've been, what we've learned about God's gifts that are made present at Advent. We said in chapter 1 that the hope God offers us is grounded in reality, that it gives us reason to look with thrilling anticipation to what's to come. And we said next that God's tender love is steadfast, that it sticks with us even when we feel like we've used up all of our second chances. And finally, we learned that God rejoices in us, and that this joy allows us to rejoice in each other, to support and be there for one another.

Knowing all of this, knowing that it can't be separated from God's other good gifts, what does the peace of Christ look like?

Oddly enough, it's very simple.

Tim Keller, senior pastor of Redeemer Church in New York City, says that a clergyperson should be able to say what the gospel is in no more than one sentence. Here's what I say: Christ has come to save and restore us and all creation. That's it. That's the gospel— the salvation and restoration of all things. And that gospel is peace.

Christ has come to save and restore us and all creation.

I say it's simple, but maybe I need to elaborate a bit more on what I just said. This gospel, this good news of peace, is expressed in Hebrew as *shalom*. God's shalom is all encompassing. It's the peace of all things. Complete wellness. Wholeness. The wholeness of knowing God's grounded hope, steadfast love, and constant joy in us and in other people. It's the wholeness that goes beyond mere circumstance, the wholeness that allows us to live in the confident knowledge that no matter what happens on a daily basis, we are part of a lasting peace that cannot be destroyed.

It's not necessarily trendy anymore, but it used to be the case that when asked how you were doing, you could say, "It's all good." I love that bit of slang. That is shalom. It's all good. To make it an even fuller statement, add "y'all." It's all good, y'all. What a beautiful theological affirmation.

LEARNING TO LIVE CHRIST'S PEACE

Peace is rooted in what you know—that it's all good, for you and for the people who know you.

But let's take this knowing a step further. Father Gregory Boyle has a saying: "No kinship, no peace. No kinship, no justice."[1] But on the other hand, if there is kinship, we will know justice. If there is kinship, we will know peace. It seems I'm complicating the issue again! What does this mean, this link between peace and justice and kinship?

Simply this: that where there is kinship, we live into our baptismal vows. Where there is the kinship born of God's peace, we resist evil, injustice, and oppression in whatever forms they present themselves, because that evil is preying upon our kin. Because in God's peace, everything is all good, we work to see that good in the world, striving to achieve the wholeness there that we've received in Christ.

---

1   Gregory Boyle, *Barking to the Choir: The Power of Radical Kinship* (New York: Simon & Schuster, 2017), 201.

You see this resistance-through-kinship at Homeboy Industries. The changes this place works in participants' lives don't just stay within its walls. One area of focus at Homeboy has been on changing thoughts within the larger society about how we deal with those who have committed crimes. Father Boyle has emphasized that instead of simply locking people up, we need to look at what's driving them to commit crimes—and then to address those causes, such as poverty and lack of opportunity.

For example, Father Boyle notes that most of the problem in his part of Los Angeles is a lack of jobs, and Homeboy works to provide those jobs. But the organization also realizes that just finding people employment won't solve lasting emotional trauma that often impairs job seekers' efforts to be successful. For young people who haven't developed the relational skills and trust necessary for attachment that most of us take for granted, building such skills is essential to keeping the jobs they've found. And so Homeboy offers services such as counseling that will help these young people to heal. It's a way of repairing harm—of restoring some justice to an unjust situation, of bringing peace into lives that have known no peace—that has influenced the way in which not only Los Angeles, but other cities around the world as well, have approached criminal justice.

Homeboy's work has convinced police to replace "the 'tough on crime' mantra that predominated in the 1980s and 1990s with a 'smart on crime' model" that aims to reduce crime through understanding and addressing the needs of underserved populations.[2]

---

2   "Why We Do It: Our History and Homeboy as a Model," Homeboy Industries, accessed June 29, 2018, https://www.homeboyindustries.org/why-we-do-it/.

It has convinced even law enforcement—a group often seen as working against the interests of certain populations—to try and reduce instances of injustice where they find them.

BRINGING IT HOME: PEACE IN SCRIPTURE

The peace of Christ that grounds Homeboy, that allows it to see good where others can't, pushes the organization to bring wholeness into the lives of others. It's what we see happening in Ephesians 2:

> *Christ is our peace. He made both Jews and Gentiles into one group. With his body, he broke down the barrier of hatred that divided us. He canceled the detailed rules of the Law so that he could create one new person out of the two groups, making peace. He reconciled them both as one body to God by the cross, which ended the hostility to God.*
>
> *When he came, he announced the good news of peace to you who were far away from God and to those who were near.*
>
> Ephesians 2:14-17

Even as Homeboy works to change society as a whole, those individual transformations keep on happening. That peace Ephesians describes has shown up in the life of a former gang member at Homeboy. Father Boyle talks about this young man's Christmas celebration. With no family, he had nowhere to go for the holiday, and no one to spend it with. But instead of killing time alone and just waiting for a potentially lonely day to come to an end, this homie decided to host dinner for six other men in the program, men he knew also had no place to go—and men who had all been his enemies. As Father Boyle tells it, the young man said, "Yeah, the seven of us, we just sat in the kitchen staring at the oven waiting for the turkey to be done." The founder of Homeboy goes on to ask about what this young man did. "So what could be more sacred than seven orphans, enemies, rivals, sitting in a kitchen waiting for a turkey to be done?"[3]

If you know kinship, you will know peace, and you will know and work for the justice that flows from this divine gift.

If you know kinship, you will know peace, and you will know and work for the justice that flows from this divine gift.

My challenge to you is that as you see injustice in the world, seek relationship with those who are being marginalized. Know and be known, and may that knowing bring God's shalom into your lives.

My prayer for us is that we would live out this good news of God announced in the birth of Christ, who has come to make things all good, y'all.

---

3   Gregory Boyle, "The Calling of Delight: Gangs, Service, and Kinship," interview by Krista Tippett, *On Being,* The On Being Project, April 2, 2015, audio, 50:59, https://onbeing.org/programs/greg-boyle-the-calling-of -delight-gangs-service-and-kinship/.

"He announced the good news of peace." Think about it: this is what so many of us do in church on Sundays, when we turn to each other and share the peace. Have you ever thought about what it means to tell your neighbor, or to receive the greeting, "The peace of Christ be with you"? I doubt any of us has ever thought this was a magical formula, meant to wipe away every last bit of unhappiness and irritation in our lives. So why do we say it?

Well, what did Jesus himself mean when he said it? You can probably remember Jesus telling someone who'd asked him for help to "go in peace." Look at Mark 5: Jesus is surrounded by a crowd, on his way to heal the daughter of Jairus, a leader in the synagogue. As they make their way to Jairus's house, Jesus notices that someone has touched him: a woman who has had a hemorrhage for twelve years, desperate for the help or cure doctors have been unable to offer her all that time. When she falls down in front of him, Jesus tells her, "Daughter, your faith has healed you; go in peace, healed from your disease" (Mark 5:34).

He does much the same thing in Luke 7, when a woman apparently known to be a sinner bursts in on a dinner Jesus has been invited to at a Pharisee's house. We're told that she washes his feet with her tears and hair, and then adds some expensive oil when she's finished. The Pharisee is horrified, but Jesus tells him that because she acted out of love to welcome him, her sins are forgiven. He then turns to the woman herself, saying, "Your faith has saved you. Go in peace" (Luke 7:50).

What was this peace Jesus assured these women of? Of course, he cured the bleeding woman of her illness—he removed the main cause of distress in her life, one that had probably driven people away from her and caused her endless amounts of worry and needless shame. And so we shouldn't be surprised that she experienced some peace, now that she was rid of the pain her illness had caused her.

The woman who was a sinner must have felt relief, too, not only at being acknowledged and treated kindly by the man she obviously revered—but at having him declare her forgiven, no matter what it was she had done that had made people look down on her, in front of a roomful of important people. Of course she must have felt an infusion of peace in her life.

But do we—did anyone—assume that these women would go through life from there on out without any problems or disappointments, any hurts or worries to disturb their perfect existence? Of course not! As is true for every human being, life is messy, in ways big and small. Maybe the woman who was a sinner would mess up again somehow; maybe someone who hadn't heard about her good fortune would continue to look down on her. Maybe the woman with a hemorrhage would get into a useless argument with a sibling or relative, and everyone would walk away feeling bad. So, no: Jesus giving peace to those he had healed didn't mean they would have a problem-free life after he blessed them. But it did do something tremendously important.

Notice that Jesus makes his declaration in front of people, in front of large crowds or dinner parties, those who know these unfortunate people in need. When he heals them and declares that peace is theirs, he's signaling to everyone around that they can no longer exclude these people from their midst. That they are and always have been part of the community, and that they are just as deserving of love and care and just plain inclusion as everyone else is. When Jesus declares that his peace is with them, he is freeing up the formerly sick or sin-laden to live in the full, messy abundance that is human life in community. He is freeing them up to experience all the everyday joys and travails that a "normal" person loves and hates; he is allowing them to live into the just plain everyday, free from the weight of condemnation that has kept them apart from the bustle and interaction that everyone else takes for granted. And just as he gives what we might want to call a normal life back to these individuals, he is also freeing the community that surrounds them to allow their fullness to blossom and to support those blossoming lives in their midst.

> **Just as [Jesus] gives what we might want to call a normal life back to these individuals, he is also freeing the community that surrounds them to allow their fullness to blossom and to support those blossoming lives in their midst.**

When all the angels declared to the shepherds, "Glory to God in heaven, and on earth peace among those whom he favors" (Luke 2:14), they just might have had in mind the work of peace that Jesus would do in his life—his granting peace to people so that they could live into the fullness of their own humanity, freed of burdens that kept them on the margins, away from people and excluded from a caring, supportive community.

Think about this meaning of peace, and then think about what happens at Homeboy. Boris, who is now a senior staff member at the center, helps newcomers get acquainted with the place and follows them through their journey, supporting them as they go along. And he knows exactly what they're going through. Bullied in elementary school, Boris joined a gang because he had no other means of protecting himself. But it wasn't easy to leave once he'd confronted his bullies. Unable to get out of the gang, he wound up serving twenty-five years in prison, hidden away from the people he loved, knowing that people viewed him as a heartless criminal no one would want in their house, feeling far removed from the everyday comforts and concerns he must have thought that the average person was lucky to experience. When Boris learned about Father Gregory Boyle, though, he was determined to be a part of Homeboy when he got out of prison. And indeed, that's right where he went when he was paroled: right into a community that accepted him, supported him, gave him opportunities, and let him grow into all the talents and desire to serve that had been tamped down in gang life and in prison, regardless of what his past had been, regardless of who else had rejected him and never given him a chance. When Boris says that Homeboy is all about spreading peace in people's lives, it sounds a lot like the peace Jesus gives to the people he's healed—according to Boris, everything about the place has been set up so that "when you walk through those doors, you automatically feel that love. Peace is the love that we bring there in the community. It's about fixing those that are broken" and "loving each other and continuing to walk that walk" together.

It's about bringing people back from the margins into the fold of community, so that they can live into the fullness of who they were intended to be. Not people without problems—but people able to handle and live through their problems because they know they are valued and supported, and because they know they can do the same for others.

And so when we tell each other in church that we wish the peace of Christ upon our neighbor, we know we're not wishing for anything impossible. Without saying it in so many words, we're saying that we're there for each other. Because Christ is there for us—for all of us—we take hold of that assurance and we spread it around in support and love: we pass the peace.

DEVOTION

Christ's gospel is peace. This is God's good news for a world that often feels less than peaceful. I don't have to recount the ways in which we see a lack of peace in our neighborhoods and in our world played out before us on the news or in social media. We sometimes experience lack of peace at work or at school. We also experience lack of peace in our homes or in our close relationships from time to time, and so we long for the realization of Christ's gospel—Christ's message of peace.

As Ephesians 2 says:

> *Christ is our peace. He made both Jews and Gentiles into one group. With his body, he broke down the barrier of hatred that divided us. He canceled the detailed rules of the Law so that he could create one new person out of the two groups, making peace. He reconciled them both as one body to God by the cross, which ended the hostility to God.*
>
> *When he came, he announced the good news of peace to you who were far away from God and to those who were near.*
>
> *Ephesians 2:14-17*

The peace that Christ offers breaks down all the walls that separate us from one another and the chains that bind us. We build up walls between us because we believe those walls will keep us safe and will give us more peace, but walls, rather than bringing more peace, often bring more fear. Christ has come to bring down barriers so that we can enter into the reconciled community of faith that God had in mind when God created us. The Triune God made us for community. Flourishing Christian community where we learn to love our neighbors as ourselves and care for one another as we pattern our lives after Christ is where we learn to share the peace of Christ.

Christ's peace is not merely contentment, it is wholeness of heart and life. Christ's peace is reconciliation. In Christ, our relationship with God and our relationships with one another are made new. In these restored relationships we discover the peace of home within the community of God.

Lord, grant us your peace. Help us to know your peace as we pray for your Kingdom to come on earth as it is in heaven. Bring peace to the places of our lives that are filled with worry, regret, and pain. As we live and move in the world, help us to be peacemakers. In the name of Jesus who is the Christ, we pray. Amen.

CONCLUSION

In those days Caesar Augustus declared that everyone throughout the empire should be enrolled in the tax lists. This first enrollment occurred when Quirinius governed Syria. Everyone went to their own cities to be enrolled. Since Joseph belonged to David's house and family line, he went up from the city of Nazareth in Galilee to David's city, called Bethlehem, in Judea. He went to be enrolled together with Mary, who was promised to him in marriage and who was pregnant. While they were there, the time came for Mary to have her baby. She gave birth to her firstborn child, a son, wrapped him snugly, and laid him in a manger, because there was no place for them in the guestroom.

Nearby shepherds were living in the fields, guarding their sheep at night. The Lord's angel stood before them, the Lord's glory shone around them, and they were terrified.

The angel said, "Don't be afraid! Look! I bring good news to you—wonderful, joyous news for all people. Your savior is born today in David's city. He is Christ the Lord. This is a sign for you: you will find a newborn baby wrapped snugly and lying in a manger." Suddenly a great assembly of the heavenly forces was with the angel praising God. They said, "Glory to God in heaven, and on earth peace among those whom he favors."

When the angels returned to heaven, the shepherds said to each other, "Let's go right now to Bethlehem and see what's happened. Let's confirm what the Lord has revealed to us." They went quickly and found Mary and Joseph, and the baby lying in the manger. When they saw this, they reported what they had been told about this child. Everyone who heard it was amazed at what the shepherds told them. Mary committed these things to memory and considered them carefully. The shepherds returned home, glorifying and praising God for all they had heard and seen. Everything happened just as they had been told.

Luke 2:1-20

We couldn't end this book without taking a final look at the hymn that's accompanied us throughout our study of Advent. Let's go back one more time to a verse from "O Holy Night":

O holy night! the stars are brightly shining;
It is the night of the dear Savior's birth.
Long lay the world in sin and error pining,
Till he appeared and the soul felt its worth.

We can imagine this holy night. The skies were serene and quiet. The stars were brightly shining, the one pointing the way north most noticeably so. Down below were a number of people earning their living off the land; shepherds were a ready audience for the miracle of Christ's birth. And as you moved in from the fields, there were all the sights and sounds of the little town of Bethlehem. Located just six miles south of Jerusalem, it was the town where David was anointed king.

You can imagine the crowded little town at the time of the census. There was no room in Bethlehem's inn for Mary and Joseph, so they camped with the livestock, and in the midst of lowing (or as we'd say today, "mooing") cattle to boot. A holy family came into existence at the birth of Jesus.

As his parents laid Jesus in a feeding trough, the angels and stars and shepherds and sheep—all of creation—bore witness to the love of God that sent Jesus to us. God had come down in the flesh—to be with *us*.

Wow, you must be pretty special for God to have done all of that.

The hymn tells us, "Long lay the world in sin and error pining." What does the song mean by that?

Pining: it's what you could describe as hanging onto the idea of something long gone, with no hope of ever seeing it return. Long lay the world yearning for something it had lost, suffering from grief and regret. Grief at its people's lack of hope for a good, or even a better, life for themselves, their loved ones, their world. Regret at having made bad decisions, at having denied someone a second chance or having not stood up for someone in need. Grief over love lost or never found, grief over the lack of joy in life. Over the inability to believe that peace can be found anywhere at all.

I know this pining world. It's a world I see every day, among people both young and old, amid the wildly successful and the down and out. Countless times, I have rehashed with others their regrets and lamented over my own. None of us is free from regret.

This is why, I think, so many people feel unworthy or worthless. We rehash the wrongs we've done, or others rehash them for us. We make "worth" synonymous with "right." If I do good— if I do and act and think in the right way—then I have worth, then I am worthy of others' love, of God's love; and if I do otherwise, I am rightfully condemned to a life without joy. If I take one wrong step, if I fall into addiction or in with the wrong crowd, I have given up any second chance—I have forever lost my worth. And so we obsess about the moral high ground, because anything less—anything broken or faulty or wrong—is worthless. Fake.

And in our darker moments, when we find ourselves in sin and error pining, we wonder: Am I worthy? We wonder: Who am I? Am I even worth loving?

> Long lay the world in sin and error pining,
> Till he appeared and the soul felt its worth.

Father Gregory Boyle says, "Sometimes you have to reach in and dismantle messages of shame and disgrace that get in the way so that the soul can feel its worth."[1] This dismantling is precisely what God set in motion at Christmas, precisely what we celebrate and anticipate during Advent: God having reached into the world in Jesus Christ to undo these narratives and their power over us, to give us a new home and new stories about who we are and were created to be, for ourselves and for each other. God reached into the world to replace these lies with divine hope, with grounded hope that can thrill in the certainty of its fulfillment. God replaced this hurt with the steadfast, tender love that never lets go, no matter how many chances we've already had. God replaced these false messages with the joy taken in us, God's creatures, and with the joy we take in each other. And God replaced our doubts about ourselves with the peace of knowing that God's hope, love, and joy will last, no matter what the issues are that we face or the changes that are taking place around us. God reached into the world through Jesus to do all of this.

Why? Because you are worth it.

By the way, if we were actually holding a party for Jesus in this season when we celebrate his birth, he'd make the entire celebration about you rather than about himself. Christ is God's gift to the world, a gift you've been given so that you will know that you in turn are a gift, not only to those around you, but even and especially to God.

---

1   Gregory Boyle, "Compassion and Kinship," TEDxConejo 2012, June 20, 2012, https://www.youtube.com/watch?v=ipR0kWt1Fkc.

My simple message to you as we approach Christmas Day is that no matter what you have done, no matter what you have done wrong, no matter how you have failed, no matter what failures may come:

God loves you. You are worth it.

> O hear the angel voices!
> O night divine, O night when Christ was born!
> O night divine!
> O night when God said: you're worth it.

For Further Study

Boyle, Gregory. *Barking to the Choir: The Power of Radical Kinship*. New York: Simon & Schuster, 2017.

———. *Tattoos on the Heart: The Power of Boundless Compassion*. New York: Free Press, 2010.

Fremon, Celeste. *G-Dog and the Homeboys: Father Greg Boyle and the Gangs of East Los Angeles*. Albuquerque: University of New Mexico Press, 2008.

G-Dog (film). Directed by Freida Lee Mock. 2013.